in just
10
minutes

For people on the go: 80 fabulous recipes for preparing great food fast

in just 10 minutes

Jenni Fleetwood

southwater

This edition is published by Southwater

Southwater is an imprint of
Anness Publishing Limited
Hermes House, 88-89 Blackfriars Road, London SE1 8HA
tel. 020 7401 2077 fax 020 7633 9499

Distributed in the UK by
The Manning Partnership
251-253 London Road East, Batheaston, Bath BA1 7RL
tel. 01225 852 727 fax 01225 852 852

Published in the USA by
Anness Publishing Inc.
27 West 20th Street, Suite 504, New York, NY 10011
fax 212 807 6813

Distributed in Australia by
Sandstone Publishing
Unit 1, 360 Norton Street, Leichhardt, New South Wales 2040
tel. 02 9560 7888 fax 02 9560 7488

All rights reserved. No part of this publication may be reproduced, stored in a retrieval system, or transmitted in any way or by any means, electronic, mechanical, photocopying, recording or otherwise, without the prior written permission of the copyright holder.

© 2001 Anness Publishing Limited

Publisher: Joanna Lorenz
Managing Editor: Linda Fraser
Senior Editor: Margaret Malone
Designer: Ian Sandom
Photography: Karl Adamson, Steve Baxter, William Lingwood, Patrick McLeavey and Tom Odulate
Recipes: Alex Barker, Kit Chan, Christine France, Sarah Gates, Shirley Gill, Soheila Kimberley, Elisabeth Lambert Ortiz, Maggie Pannell and Hilaire Walden

Previously published as part of a larger compendium, *The Ultimate 30 Minute Cookbook*

1 3 5 7 9 10 8 6 4 2

NOTES

Bracketed terms are intended for American readers. For all recipes, quantities are given in both metric and imperial measures and, where appropriate, measures are also given in standard cups and spoons. Follow one set, but not a mixture because they are not interchangeable. Medium (US large) eggs are used unless otherwise stated. Standard spoon and cup measures are level. 1 tsp = 5ml, 1 tbsp = 15ml, 1 cup = 250ml/8fl oz
Australian standard tablespoons are 20ml. Australian readers should use 3 tsp in place of 1 tbsp for measuring small quantities of gelatine, cornflour, salt etc.

CONTENTS

Introduction *6*

Quick-cooking Techniques *10*

Mix and Match Menus *12*

10 MINUTE RECIPES *14*

Soups, Appetizers and Snacks *16*

Poultry and Meat Dishes *34*

Fish and Seafood Dishes *45*

Pasta *52*

Salads and Vegetable Dishes *60*

Desserts *82*

Index *96*

INTRODUCTION

Today's hectic lifestyle means that most people have less and less time to spend in the kitchen. After a hard day, either at work or at home, few of us feel inclined to spend hours slaving over a hot stove – or even a hot microwave. Paradoxically, however, we do all want interesting, well presented, healthy meals that are colourful and full of flavour.

So what's the solution? Do you pop into your nearest supermarket and stock up on those expensive ready-prepared meals or do you build up a repertoire of fast, easy dishes that can be made in the brief moments between getting in from work or returning from the school run and whizzing out again?

That's where we come in. For this book, we've assembled as fine a collection of quick cook recipes as you could find anywhere. Every recipe in the book can be completed in just ten minutes – and you can't say fairer than that.

Of course, precisely how long each dish will actually take depends on a number of factors: the competence of the cook; the distractions (children, pets, partners); and how many glasses of wine are consumed in the process. Some dishes benefit from being chilled or marinated if time permits, but when time is short, simply skip these options.

Preparation and cooking times for each recipe are given as a guide. Where these are inextricably linked, as when the cook puts on a pan of pasta, then uses the time while it cooks to prepare the vegetables for a sauce, for example, a combined time is given.

Master a few favourite recipes and you're ready for the next challenge – the under-ten-minute menu! Some suggestions for mix-and-match dishes are given in the pages that follow, together with techniques for basic recipes that are infinitely adaptable.

PLANNING AHEAD
Before starting, ask yourself three questions. How much time and energy do I have? What ingredients do I have in the refrigerator? What is the quickest way I can turn time, energy and ingredient into a satisfying meal? It might help to develop a strategy on paper that shows exactly what you are cooking, what shopping you need and where you have to go to get it.

When even the simplest meals are properly thought out, three quarters of the work is done. From your list you will know exactly what you are cooking, what shopping you need, where to get it from and what you are going to do with the ingredients when you start to get to work in the kitchen.

It is always worth taking a few minutes to read a recipe through before you start. This will enable you to have all the necessary equipment to hand from the outset. Many cooks work best of all in a slightly creative mess where somehow everything comes together in the end. Whatever state you are comfortable with, make sure things are "just so" before you begin cooking.

Left: Quick-cook savoury staples include flour, dried pulses, bottled and canned capers, tomatoes and vegetables, fresh fruit and vegetables, wine, oils and vinegars, garlic, fresh herbs, and eggs.

Above: Ideal as a treat, take-away food, often high in fat and sugar, soon loses its appeal.

QUICK-COOK SHORT CUTS

The canny cook cheats. Digging your own potatoes or picking and podding your own peas are both admirable pursuits, but for fabulous fast food what you really need is a first class supermarket, which will do the hard work for you. It is now possible to buy a huge range of fresh produce that is ready to cook, from trimmed fine beans and mangetouts (snow peas) to carrot batons and sliced leeks. Look out for ready-sliced, fresh pineapple, mango and melon – fresh and tasty, without the fuss.

Salad leaves are available in astonishing variety – not cheap, but wonderfully convenient – and there's an equally wide range of ready-made dressings and sauces, if you can't spare a few minutes to make one of your own.

Right: Store-cupboard (pantry) essentials for desserts include sugar, cocoa powder, chocolate sauce, meringues, fresh fruit, biscuits (cookies), nuts and canned fruits.

If it's medleys you're after, you'll find them too. Packets of prepared mixed vegetables are widely available, and where once you would be lucky to find a single stir-fry mix, there are now a whole range of Asian mixtures. The stir-fry vegetables may even come with a sauce, so for a quick main course, just add strips of chicken breast.

If meat is to be cooked very quickly, it must be tender. Turkey escalopes (US scallops) are ideal, especially if they are beaten out thinly, then crumbed or simply cooked in a tasty sauce. Calf's or lamb's liver is equally appropriate, and has the added advantage of being a good source of iron.

Fish is the original fast food: skinned fillets need no preparation and cook extremely quickly, as does shellfish. The well-stocked pantry should include cans of tuna, anchovies and salmon – all staples that can be used to create quick meals.

So – next stop, the grocery section. Even here, there has been a revolution. Once upon a time, canned tomatoes meant whole fruits in a thin, pippy liquid. Today, the tomatoes are often chopped, and you can get them with herbs, garlic, (bell) peppers and chillies. Passata (bottled sieved tomatoes), which is sold in jars or cans, and tubes of tomato paste or garlic paste, are equally useful.

Also invaluable are cans or jars of fruit, pimientos, chillies, artichoke hearts, beans and other pulses, pesto and olive tapenade. Of course, some of these ingredients cost a little more, but convenience never comes without a price.

From the chiller cabinet, you'll need fresh eggs, cream, yogurt, cheeses, butter and margarine, and pastry.

What else? Obviously, you'll need all the staples like flour, sugar, raising agents and rice. Trifle sponges, boudoir biscuits (cookies) and slabs of gingerbread are first steps to simple desserts, and ready-to-top pizza bases and tortillas also save time.

When it comes to pasta, buy the fresh product if possible, as it not only tastes superb but also cooks in just a few minutes. Dried pasta that cooks in under ten minutes is readily available.

This book is very much in line with modern trends in cooking. Ready-meal dishes remain a mainstay for many busy families, but there has been a swing back to "real" food. We may have neither the time nor the inclination to spend hours on complicated cooking procedures, but we still want to watch food cooking, relish the aromas, hear the meat sizzle in the pan. This collection of recipes promises all that – and in next to no time.

ADDING FLAVOURS

Of course, if cooking is reduced to putting together assorted packages, it isn't very satisfying. The trick is to add extra ingredients of your own to give the dish a unique signature. Herbs, spices, sauces and flavourings can make the difference between a disappointingly average dish and one that has everyone begging for the recipe.

Above: There are any number of spices and flavourings that will give instant zing to dishes.

Herbs and spices give different, subtle and unusual flavours to many dishes. Fresh are nicer in raw, salad-type dishes but dried are fine for cooked dishes. Dried herbs are stronger than fresh ones, so do not overdo when using them in cooking.

Garlic, chives and peppercorns, to name just a few, are wonderful flavourings. Garlic can be used raw or cooked. Ginger, both fresh and dried, is also a hugely useful spice. It will give a lift to meats and most vegetables. Cinnamon, nutmeg and cloves are ideal for adding flavours to fruit and ice cream for simple, delicious desserts.

Don't forget ingredients such as olives, capers, nuts and seeds for quick ways to add texture, colour and flavour to dishes.

Left: Often overlooked, olives, nuts and capers add crunch to a salad, and are delicious on their own.

EQUIPMENT

Stocking up on every item in your local cookware shop will not make you a better or faster cook, but some basic items are definitely worth investing in.

A few good pans in various sizes and with tight-fitting lids are a must. Heavy-based and non-stick pans are best. A large frying pan is invaluable for the quick cook. The food cooks faster when spread over a wider surface area. For the same reason, a good wok is essential. Use either a large pan or frying pan when a recipe calls for occasional stirring, and a wok for continuous movement, such as stir-frying.

Good quality knives can halve your preparation time, but more importantly, a really sharp knife is safer than a blunt one. You can do yourself a lot of damage if your hand slips when you are pressing down hard with a blunt knife. For basic, day-to-day use choose a good chopping knife, a small vegetable knife and a long serrated bread knife. If possible store knives safely in well-secured slotted racks. Drawer storage is not good for knives as the blades can easily become damaged when they are knocked around. If you do have to keep knives in a drawer, make sure they are stored with their handles towards the front for safe lifting and keep the blades protected in some way. Good sharp knives are essential pieces of kitchen equipment, so it is worth taking care of them.

Other essential pieces of equipment include chopping boards, a colander, a sieve, a grater, and whisk.

For the cook who likes to cook speedily and efficiently, where you store your equipment is an important factor to consider. Many cooks use the stove as the pivot around which most of the action takes place. Pots, pans, whisks, spoons and strainers can hang overhead, a chopping board is on an adjacent work surface and pots hold a variety of wooden spoons, fish slices (spatulas), ladles, scissors, peelers and other kitchen utensils, all within easy reach.

Below: Equipment essentials for speedy and safe cooking.

Quick-cook Basic Recipes

Every quick cook needs a few basics that can be mixed and matched to make a meal in moments. In the savoury stakes, the prime candidate has to be tomato sauce. Its uses are so many that it is included here even though it will take you more than ten minutes to prepare. The beauty of this sauce, however, is that it can be made in advance and kept in the refrigerator for up to seven days, which will allow you to save precious time when cooking.

Garlic Oil

> Preparation time 1–2 minutes
> Cooking time Nil

MAKES 120ML/4FL OZ/½ CUP
6–8 garlic cloves
120ml/4fl oz/½ cup olive oil

1. Trim the root end from the garlic cloves. Tap each clove sharply under the side of a large knife, banging with a fist until the clove splits and the skin loosens. Discard the skin.

2. Use the back of a heavy knife, near the handle, to crush the garlic. Hold the knife firmly, secure the clove carefully with your thumb and forefinger, then crush with a chopping motion.

3. Transfer the crushed garlic into a screw-topped jar, cover fully with olive oil and store at room temperature. The oil will keep for up to two weeks. Use for cooking and in dressings and sauces.

Tomato Sauce

> Preparation time 10 minutes
> Cooking time 20 minutes

MAKES ABOUT 300ML/½ PINT/1¼ CUPS
15ml/1 tbsp olive oil
1 onion, finely chopped
1 garlic clove, crushed
400g/14oz can chopped tomatoes
15ml/1 tbsp tomato purée (paste)
15ml/1 tbsp chopped fresh mixed herbs
pinch of sugar
salt and ground black pepper

1. Heat the oil in a pan, add the onion and garlic and fry over a gentle heat for 5 minutes, stirring occasionally, until softened.

2. Add the tomatoes, then stir in the tomato purée, fresh mixed herbs, sugar and salt and ground black pepper to taste.

3. Bring to the boil, then simmer, uncovered, over a medium heat for about 15 minutes, stirring occasionally, until the mixture has reduced to a thick pulp. Leave to cool, then cover the sauce and chill until ready to use.

Cooking Pasta

> Preparation time Nil
> Cooking time 3–10 minutes

SERVES 4
350g/12oz pasta
salt
30ml/2 tbsp olive oil or a knob (pat) of butter, to serve

1. Bring a large pan of lightly salted water to the boil. Add the pasta and stir to separate the strands or shapes.

2. Cook at a rolling boil until the pasta is tender but still firm to the bite. When halved, shapes must be cooked through.

3. Drain the pasta well in a colander, shaking it hard to remove the excess water. Tip into a bowl and add a drizzle of olive oil or a knob of butter and then scatter over a little grated Parmesan or add your favourite sauce.

> ### Cook's Tip
> Always cook pasta in plenty of water in a large pan to prevent it from sticking.

Three more great basics: a good salad dressing can double up as an effective baste for the grill (broiler) and barbecue. This dressing is delicious with white meats as well as fish. Chocolate sauce or raspberry purée can be used to top ice cream, meringues or fruit. Raspberry purée is also delicious spooned over slices of brioche that have been soaked in egg and cream, then fried in butter.

Salad Dressing or Baste

Preparation time 2 minutes
Cooking time Nil

MAKES 105ML/7 TBSP
90ml/6 tbsp olive oil
15ml/1 tbsp white wine vinegar
5ml/1 tsp French mustard
½ garlic clove, crushed
1.5ml/¼ tsp sugar

1 Pour the oil and vinegar into a screw-topped jar. Add the mustard, garlic and sugar.

2 Shake well, and use as a dressing for salads or marinade for meat and fish. Store the dressing in the refrigerator. Do not keep for longer than two weeks.

Chocolate Sauce

Preparation time 1 minute
Cooking time 5 minutes

MAKES 250ML/8FL OZ/1 CUP
150ml/¼ pint/⅔ cup single (light) cream
15ml/1 tbsp caster (superfine) sugar
150g/5oz best quality plain (semisweet) chocolate, broken
30ml/2 tbsp dark rum or whisky (optional)

1 Rinse out a small pan with cold water to prevent the sauce from catching on the bottom. Pour in the cream, stir in the sugar and bring to the boil over a medium heat.

2 Remove the pan from the heat and add the chocolate, a few pieces at a time, stirring after each addition until the chocolate has melted and the sauce is smooth. Stir in the rum or whisky, if using.

3 Pour the chocolate sauce into a jug (pitcher) and use immediately. Alternatively, pour it into a clean jar and cool quickly. Close the jar and store the sauce in the refrigerator for up to 10 days.

Raspberry Purée

Preparation time 1–2 minutes
Cooking time 1–5 minutes

1 Hull, clean and dry fresh raspberries and place them in a blender or food processor. Pulse the machine a few times, scraping down the sides of the bowl once or twice, until the berries form a purée.

2 If using frozen raspberries, put them in a pan with a little sugar and place over a gentle heat to soften and release the juices. Simmer for 5 minutes, then cool.

3 Press the purée through a fine-mesh sieve (strainer) to remove any fibres or seeds. Sweeten with icing (confectioners') sugar and sharpen the flavour with lemon juice or a fruit-flavour liqueur, to taste.

Cook's Tip
Other soft summer fruits can be used to make a purée; try strawberries or blueberries, which can be puréed raw, or peaches, apricots or nectarines, which should first be poached lightly.

Mix and Match Menus

You can produce an entire meal in an amazingly short amount of time if you mix and match carefully. Choose one dish that needs to stand or can be left to cook for a few minutes, during which time you can put together a salad or speedy dessert. These flexible menus include recipes from the book and some simple ideas for which no recipe is needed.

Teenagers' Treat

Guacamole can be made in moments and is delicious with either spicy tortilla chips or crisp vegetable dippers.

Save time and effort by getting each guest to top his or her own Ciabatta bread pizza.

Instant salad: Mix bought ready-washed mixed salad leaves with sliced avocado, red onion, orange segments and walnuts.

Ice Cream Strawberry Shortcake is a quick and simple assembly job that is best done at the last minute.

Family Favourite

Melting Cheese Dip is always a hit with friends and family. Serve with crusty bread or spicy sausage for extra flavour.

Cashew Chicken couldn't be easier. Cook quickly on a high heat for maximum flavour and texture.

Chopped salad vegetables with crumbled feta cheese and olives make Turkish Salad a flavourful accompaniment. Add the dressing at the last moment.

For a final flourish, serve Quick Apricot Blender Whip for a colourful and light dessert.

Sophisticated Supper

Sautéed Scallops are very quick and easy, so prepare them ahead if you like, but cook them at the very last minute.

Pan-fried Veal Chops is a good main course; make the sauce while cooking the scallops.

As an accompaniment, serve crusty bread or rolls and Citrus Green Leaf Salad, omitting the croûtons if time is very short.

There's no time left to make an elaborate dessert, so simply serve fresh raspberries or strawberries with a dollop of cream.

Mix and Match Menus

Vegetarian Feast

Make an easy appetizer by serving warm focaccia bread with sea salt crystals and olives.

Ravioli with Four-cheese Sauce can easily be cooked at the same time as the tomatoes are cooking.

Garlic Topped Tomatoes bring colour and taste to any menu: top halved tomatoes with crushed garlic, a little softened butter and salt and grill (broil) for 5–7 minutes until golden on top.

Finally, assemble Figs with Ricotta Cream while the main-course dishes are cooking.

Party Time

Quick suggestions for party food: Serve Hummus with pitta bread instead of toast.

Tomato and Mozzarella Toasts resemble mini pizzas and are perfect for parties.

Deep-fried Whitebait has a spicy coating which gives them a pleasantly crunchy taste. Serve in Mediterranean-style platters for a sun-filled feel to your next party.

Make miniature Asparagus Rolls wrapped in strips of prosciutto ham and serve with a ready-made mayonnaise dip.

Light Lunch

Melon and Grapefruit Cocktail is a cool and refreshing appetizer without being filling.

Salmon with Green Peppercorns is a good light main course and needs very little attention during cooking.

While the salmon is cooking, toss together Frisée Lettuce Salad with Bacon and spicy mustard dressing to serve as a tasty accompaniment.

Brazilian Coffee Bananas is one of the easiest desserts. Make it just before serving. Use nut-flavoured yogurt in place of the Greek (US strained plain) yogurt, if you like.

10 MINUTE RECIPES

If you only have ten minutes to spare, take the fast track. Simple soups like Avgolemono get you off to a racing start, as do appetizers like Smoked Trout Salad or Prosciutto with Mango. Take a tip from the tapas table and try Garlic Prawns or Chorizo in Olive Oil. Want something substantial as well as speedy? Pork with Camembert is just the ticket. And for the grand finale, Chocolate Fudge Sundaes or Brazilian Coffee Bananas will have everyone cheering.

Avgolemono

This is the most popular of Greek soups. The name means egg and lemon, the two important ingredients, which produce a light, nourishing soup. Orzo is Greek, rice-shaped pasta, but you can use any small pasta shapes.

Preparation time 2 minutes
Cooking time 5 minutes

SERVES 4–6
1.75 litres/3 pints/7½ cups chicken stock
115g/4oz/1 cup orzo pasta
3 eggs
juice of 1 large lemon
salt and ground black pepper
lemon slices, to garnish

1 Pour the stock into a large pan, and bring to the boil. Add the pasta and cook for 5 minutes.

2 Beat the eggs until frothy, then add the lemon juice and 15ml/1 tbsp of cold water. Slowly stir in a ladleful of the hot chicken stock, then add one or two more. Remove the pan from the heat, return this mixture to it and stir well. Season with salt and pepper and serve immediately, garnished with lemon slices. Do not let the soup boil once the eggs have been added or it will curdle.

COOK'S TIPS
Good-quality chicken stock is the secret of this speedy recipe. Look out for cartons of stock in the chilled cabinet of your local supermarket, or buy canned bouillon.

Making your own stock may sound like a chore, but if you recycle the meaty carcass of a roast chicken, it can be prepared in less time than it takes to clear the table after Sunday lunch.

Just pop the carcass in a pan, add an onion, a carrot and a bouquet garni, pour over water to cover generously and bring it to the boil. Lower the heat to the lowest setting, cover the pan and leave the stock to simmer for about 2 hours or until the aroma reminds you it is time to turn it off.

Strain the stock into a bowl, cool it quickly, then skim off any fat from the surface. Chicken stock freezes well for up to 3 months and should be seasoned on thawing.

THAI-STYLE CORN SOUP

This is a very quick and easy soup. If you are using frozen prawns, thaw them first.

Preparation time 3 minutes
Cooking time 5 minutes

SERVES 4

2.5ml/ ½ tsp sesame or sunflower oil
2 spring onions (scallions),
  thinly sliced
1 garlic clove, crushed
600ml/1 pint/2½ cups chicken stock
425g/15oz can creamed corn
225g/8oz/1¼ cups cooked,
  peeled prawns (shrimp)
5ml/1 tsp green chilli paste (optional)
salt and ground black pepper
fresh coriander (cilantro) leaves,
  to garnish

1. Heat the oil in a large heavy pan and sauté the spring onions and garlic over a medium heat, until softened.

2. Stir in the chicken stock, creamed corn, prawns and chilli paste, if using.

3. Bring the soup to the boil, stirring occasionally. Season with salt and ground black pepper to taste, then serve at once, sprinkling with fresh coriander leaves to garnish.

COOK'S TIP
If creamed corn is not available, use ordinary canned sweetcorn, puréed in a food processor for a few seconds, until the mixture is creamy yet retains some texture.

VARIATIONS
To make Thai-style Crab and Corn Soup, use canned or freshly cooked crab in place of all or some of the cooked, peeled prawns.

Pan-fried Chicken Liver Salad

This Florentine salad uses vin santo, a delicious sweet dessert wine from Tuscany, but this is not essential — any dessert wine will do, or a sweet or cream sherry.

Preparation time 4 minutes
Cooking time 6 minutes

SERVES 4

75g/3oz fresh baby spinach leaves
75g/3oz lollo rosso leaves
75ml/5 tbsp olive oil
15g/ ½oz/1 tbsp butter
225g/8oz chicken livers, trimmed and thinly sliced
45ml/3 tbsp vin santo
50–75g/2–3oz fresh Parmesan cheese, shaved into curls
salt and ground black pepper

1 Wash and dry the spinach and lollo rosso. Tear the leaves into a large bowl, season with salt and ground black pepper to taste and toss gently to mix.

2 Heat 30ml/2 tbsp of the oil with the butter in a large heavy frying pan. When foaming, add the chicken livers and toss over a medium to high heat for 5 minutes or until the livers are browned on the outside but still pink in the centre. Remove from the heat.

3 Remove the livers from the pan with a slotted spoon, drain them on kitchen paper, then place on top of the salad leaves.

4 Return the pan to a medium heat, add the remaining oil and the vin santo and stir until sizzling. Pour the hot dressing over the leaves and chicken livers and toss to coat. Put the salad in a serving bowl and sprinkle over the Parmesan shavings. Serve immediately.

Deep-Fried Whitebait

The spicy coating on these fish gives this fast favourite a crunchy bite.

Preparation time 2 minutes
Cooking time 7–8 minutes

SERVES 6

115g/4oz/1 cup plain (all-purpose) flour
2.5ml/½ tsp curry powder
2.5ml/½ tsp ground ginger
2.5ml/½ tsp ground cayenne pepper
pinch of salt
1.2kg/2½lb fresh whitebait
vegetable oil, for deep-frying
lemon wedges, to garnish

1 Sift the flour into a bowl and stir in the curry powder, ground ginger, cayenne and salt.

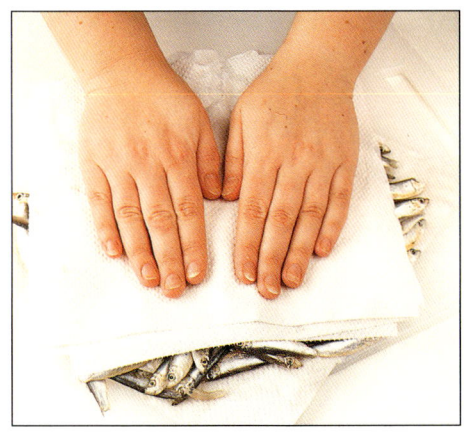

2 Lay two sheets of kitchen paper on the work surface. Spread out the whitebait on top, then cover with more kitchen paper. Blot the fish thoroughly to dry them.

3 Add a few whitebait at a time to the seasoned flour and stir gently until they are evenly coated. Heat the vegetable oil in a large, heavy pan until it reaches a temperature of 190°C/375°F.

4 Fry the whitebait in batches for 2–3 minutes until the fish is golden and crispy. Drain well on kitchen paper, keeping each batch hot while cooking the next. Serve hot garnished with lemon wedges.

MELON AND GRAPEFRUIT COCKTAIL

This pretty, colourful appetizer is perfect for all those occasions when you don't have much time for cooking, but want something really special to eat.

Preparation time 8 minutes
Cooking time Nil

SERVES 4
1 small canteloupe or Ogen melon
1 small Charentais melon
2 pink grapefruit
45ml/3 tbsp orange juice
60ml/4 tbsp red vermouth
seeds from ½ pomegranate
mint sprigs, to garnish

COOK'S TIP
To check if the melons are ripe, smell them – they should have a heady aroma, and give slightly when pressed gently at the stalk end.

1. Halve the melons lengthways and scoop out all the seeds. Cut into wedges and remove the skins, then cut across into large bite-size pieces. Set the melon aside.

2. Using a small sharp knife, cut the peel and pith from the grapefruit. Holding the fruit over a bowl to catch the juice, cut between the grapefruit membranes to release the segments.

3. Stir the orange juice and vermouth into the reserved grapefruit juice.

4. Arrange the melon pieces and grapefruit segments on four individual serving plates. Spoon over the dressing, then scatter with the pomegranate seeds. Garnish with mint sprigs.

PROSCIUTTO WITH MANGO

Other fresh, colourful fruits, such as figs, papaya or melon would go equally well with the prosciutto in this light, elegant first course. It is amazingly simple to prepare and can be made in advance – ideal if you are serving a complicated main course.

Preparation time 5 minutes
Cooking time Nil

SERVES 4
12 slices prosciutto
1 ripe mango
ground black pepper
flat leaf parsley sprigs, to garnish

1. Separate the prosciutto slices and arrange three on each of four individual plates, crumpling the prosciutto slightly to create a decorative effect.

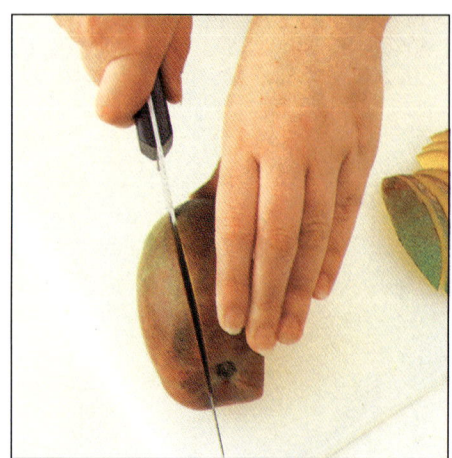

2. Cut the mango flesh off the stone (pit), then slice and peel.

3. Just before serving, arrange the mango slices in among the ham. Grind over some black pepper or offer this at the table. Garnish with flat leaf parsley sprigs.

Chorizo in Olive Oil

Spanish chorizo sausage has a deliciously pungent taste; its robust seasoning of garlic, chilli and paprika flavours the ingredients it is cooked with. Frying chorizo with onions and olive oil is one of its simplest and most delicious uses.

Preparation time 2 minutes
Cooking time 7–8 minutes

SERVES 4
75ml/5 tbsp extra virgin olive oil
350g/12oz chorizo sausage, sliced
1 large onion, thinly sliced
roughly chopped flat leaf parsley, to garnish
warm bread, to serve

1. Heat the oil in a frying pan and fry the chorizo slices over a high heat until they begin to colour. Lift out with a slotted spoon.

2. Add the onion to the pan and fry until coloured. Return the sausage slices to the pan and heat through for 1 minute.

3. Tip the mixture into a shallow serving dish and sprinkle with the parsley. Serve with warm bread.

Variation
Chorizo is usually available in large supermarkets or delicatessens. Other similarly rich, spicy sausages can be used as a substitute.

Garlic Prawns

For this simple Spanish tapas dish, you really need fresh raw prawns that will absorb the flavours of the garlic and chilli as they fry. Have everything ready for last-minute cooking so that you can take it to the table still sizzling.

Preparation time 5 minutes
Cooking time 5 minutes

SERVES 4
350–450g/12oz–1lb large raw prawns (shrimp)
2 red chillies
75ml/5 tbsp olive oil
3 garlic cloves, crushed
salt and ground black pepper

1. Remove the heads and shells from the prawns, leaving the tails intact.

2. Halve each chilli lengthways and discard the seeds. Heat the oil in a flameproof pan, suitable for serving. (Alternatively, use a frying pan and have a warmed serving dish ready in the oven.)

3. Add all the prawns, chillies and garlic to the pan and cook over a high heat for about 3 minutes, stirring until the prawns turn pink. Season lightly with salt and ground black pepper and serve immediately.

Melon, Pineapple and Grape Cocktail

A light fresh fruit salad, with no added sugar, makes a refreshing and speedy starter.

Preparation time 6 minutes
Cooking time Nil

SERVES 4
½ melon
225g/8oz fresh pineapple
225g/8oz seedless white grapes, halved
120ml/4fl oz/ ½ cup white grape juice
fresh mint leaves, to garnish

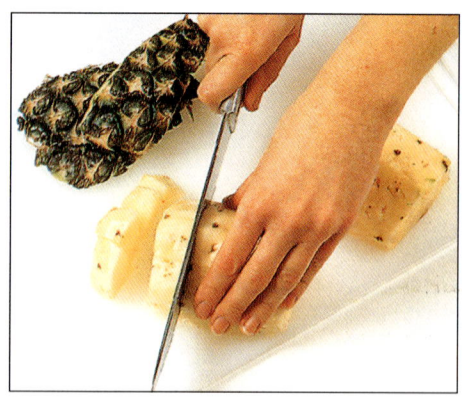

1 Remove the seeds from the melon half and use a melon baller to scoop out even-size balls.

2 Using a sharp knife, cut the skin from the pineapple. Cut the fruit into bite-size chunks.

3 Combine all the fruits in a glass serving dish and pour over the white grape juice. Serve immediately or cover and chill until required. Garnish with mint leaves.

Cook's Tip
To save even more time, use a 225g/8oz can of pineapple chunks in natural juice. Drain the chunks, reserving the juice in a measuring jug (cup). Make it up to the required quantity for pouring over the fruit with white grape juice.

SMOKED TROUT SALAD

Horseradish is as good a partner to smoked trout as it is to roast beef. Here it is combined with yogurt to make a light salad dressing.

Preparation time 6 minutes
Cooking time Nil

SERVES 4
1 oakleaf or other red lettuce
225g/8oz small tomatoes, cut into thin wedges
½ cucumber, peeled and thinly sliced
4 smoked trout fillets, about 200g/7oz each, skinned and flaked

FOR THE DRESSING
pinch of English (hot) mustard powder
15–20ml/3–4 tsp white wine vinegar
30ml/2 tbsp light olive oil
100ml/3½fl oz/scant ½ cup natural (plain) yogurt
about 30ml/2 tbsp grated fresh or bottled horseradish
pinch of caster (superfine) sugar

[1] First, make the dressing. Mix together the mustard powder and vinegar, then gradually whisk in the oil, yogurt, horseradish and sugar.

VARIATION
This salad is equally good with smoked mackerel. Add a garnish of lime or orange slices, slit to the centre and twisted.

[2] Place the lettuce leaves in a large bowl. Stir the dressing again, then pour half of it over the leaves and toss lightly.

[3] Arrange the lettuce on four individual plates with the tomatoes, cucumber and trout. Spoon over the remaining dressing and serve immediately.

Hot Tomato and Mozzarella Salad

A quick, easy dish with a wonderful Mediterranean flavour. It can be prepared in advance, chilled, then cooked just before serving.

Preparation time 5 minutes
Cooking time 4–5 minutes

SERVES 4

450g/1lb plum tomatoes, sliced
225g/8oz mozzarella cheese, sliced
1 red onion, finely chopped
4–6 pieces sun-dried tomatoes in oil, drained and chopped
60ml/4 tbsp olive oil
5ml/1 tsp red wine vinegar
2.5ml/ ½ tsp Dijon mustard
60ml/4 tbsp chopped fresh mixed herbs, such as basil, parsley, oregano and chives
salt and ground black pepper
fresh herb sprigs, to garnish (optional)

1 Arrange the sliced tomatoes and mozzarella in concentric circles in four individual shallow flameproof dishes.

2 Sprinkle over the chopped onion and sun-dried tomatoes. Preheat the grill (broiler) to high.

3 Whisk together the olive oil, vinegar, mustard, chopped herbs and seasoning. Pour over the salads.

4 Place the salads under the hot grill for 4–5 minutes, until the mozzarella starts to melt. Grind over plenty of black pepper and serve immediately, garnished with fresh herb sprigs, if liked.

Asparagus with Tarragon Butter

Eating fresh asparagus with your fingers can be messy, but it is the only proper way to eat it!

Preparation time 2 minutes
Cooking time 6–8 minutes

SERVES 4

500g/1¼ lb fresh asparagus
115g/4oz/ ½ cup butter
30ml/2 tbsp chopped fresh tarragon
15ml/1 tbsp chopped fresh parsley, plus extra to garnish
grated rind of ½ lemon
15ml/1 tbsp lemon juice
salt and ground black pepper

Cook's Tip
When buying fresh asparagus, choose spears that are plump and have a good even colour with tightly budded tips. The best asparagus is home-grown, as it starts to lose its flavour when cut.

1 Trim the woody ends from the asparagus spears, then tie them into four equal bundles.

2 Place the bundles of asparagus in a large frying pan with about 2.5cm/1in boiling water. Cover and cook for about 6–8 minutes, until the asparagus is tender but still firm. Drain well and discard the strings.

3 Meanwhile, melt the butter in a small pan. Add the tarragon, parsley, lemon rind and juice.

4 Arrange the asparagus spears on four warmed serving plates. Season the hot tarragon butter with salt and pepper, pour it over the asparagus and serve immediately. Garnish with chopped parsley.

Guacamole

Nachos or tortilla chips are the perfect accompaniment for this classic Mexican dip.

Preparation time 5 minutes
Cooking time Nil

SERVES 4
2 ripe avocados
2 red chillies, seeded
1 garlic clove
1 shallot
30ml/2 tbsp olive oil, plus extra to serve
juice of 1 lemon
salt
flat leaf parsley leaves, to garnish

1. Halve the avocados, remove their stones (pits) and scoop out their flesh into a bowl.

2. Mash the flesh well with a large fork or a potato masher.

3. Finely chop the chillies, garlic and shallot, then stir into the mashed avocado with the olive oil and lemon juice. Add salt to taste.

4. Spoon the mixture into a small serving bowl. Drizzle over a little olive oil and scatter with a few flat leaf parsley leaves. Serve.

HUMMUS

Serve this nutritious dip with vegetable crudités for a simple and satisfying appetizer or spread it on hot buttered toast.

Preparation time 5 minutes
Cooking time 2–3 minutes

SERVES 4

400g/14oz can chickpeas, drained
2 garlic cloves
30ml/2 tbsp tahini or unsweetened smooth peanut butter
60ml/4 tbsp olive oil
juice of 1 lemon
2.5ml/½ tsp cayenne pepper
15ml/1 tbsp sesame seeds
sea salt

1. Rinse the chickpeas well and place in a blender or food processor with the garlic and a good pinch of sea salt.

2. Add the tahini or peanut butter and process until fairly smooth. With the motor still running, slowly pour in the oil and lemon juice.

COOK'S TIP
Tahini is a thick, smooth and oily paste made from sesame seeds. It is available from health food shops and large supermarkets. Tahini is a classic ingredient in hummus, this Middle-Eastern dip; peanut butter would not be used in a traditional recipe, but it is a useful substitute.

3. Stir in the cayenne pepper and add more salt, to taste. If the mixture is too thick, stir in a little cold water. Transfer the purée to a serving bowl.

4. Heat a small non-stick pan and add the sesame seeds. Cook for 2–3 minutes, shaking the pan, until the seeds are golden. Allow to cool, then sprinkle over the purée.

Melting Cheese Dip

This is a classic fondue in true Swiss style. It should be served with cubes of crusty, day-old bread, but it is also good with chunks of spicy, cured sausage, such as chorizo.

Preparation time 3 minutes
Cooking time 7 minutes

SERVES 2

1 garlic clove, finely chopped
150ml/ ¼ pint/ ⅔ cup dry white wine
150g/5oz Gruyère cheese
15ml/1 tbsp Kirsch
5ml/1 tsp cornflour (cornstarch)
salt and ground black pepper
bread or chorizo cubes, to serve

1. Place the garlic and wine in a small pan and bring gently to the boil. Lower the heat and simmer for 3–4 minutes.

COOK'S TIP
Gruyère is a tasty cheese that melts incredibly well. Don't substitute other cheeses in this dip.

2. Coarsely grate the cheese and stir it into the wine. Continue to stir as the cheese melts.

3. Blend the Kirsch and cornflour to a paste and pour into the pan, stirring. Bring to the boil, stirring constantly until the sauce is smooth and thickened.

4. Add salt and pepper to taste. Serve immediately in heated bowls or transfer to a fondue pan and keep hot over a spirit burner. Garnish with black pepper and serve with bread or chorizo cubes speared on fondue forks.

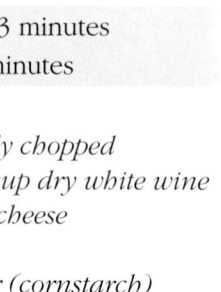

CIABATTA WITH MOZZARELLA AND ONION

Ciabatta is readily available in most supermarkets. It's even more delicious when made with spinach, sun-dried tomatoes or olives, and you'll probably find these in your local delicatessen.

Preparation time 3 minutes
Cooking time 7 minutes

MAKES 4
1 ciabatta loaf
60ml/4 tbsp red pesto
2 small mild onions
oil, for brushing
225g/8oz mozzarella cheese
8 black olives

1. Preheat the grill (broiler) to high. Cut the bread in half horizontally and toast lightly. Spread with the red pesto.

VARIATIONS
Toast halved baguettes and top with sliced cherry tomatoes and goat's cheese, then grill (broil) and garnish with shredded fresh basil.

Toast halved French sticks, spread with passata (tomato purée) and top with slices of mozzarella, anchovies and black olives, then grill and garnish with fresh oregano leaves.

2. Peel the onions and cut them horizontally into thick slices. Brush with oil and grill for about 3 minutes until lightly browned.

3. Slice the cheese and arrange over the bread. Lay the onion slices on top and sprinkle some olives over. Cut in half diagonally. Place under a hot grill for 2–3 minutes until the cheese melts.

SALAD LEAVES WITH GORGONZOLA

Crispy fried pancetta makes a tasty addition and contrasts well in texture and flavour with the softness of mixed salad leaves and the sharp taste of Gorgonzola. If pancetta is not available, use unsmoked streaky bacon instead.

Preparation time 5 minutes
Cooking time 5 minutes

SERVES 4

225g/8oz pancetta rashers (strips), rinds removed, coarsely chopped
2 large garlic cloves, roughly chopped
75g/3oz rocket (arugula) leaves
75g/3oz radicchio leaves
50g/2oz/ ½ cup walnuts, roughly chopped
115g/4oz Gorgonzola cheese
60ml/4 tbsp olive oil
15ml/1 tbsp balsamic vinegar
salt and ground black pepper

1 Put the chopped pancetta and garlic in a non-stick or heavy frying pan and heat gently, stirring constantly, until the pancetta fat runs. Increase the heat and fry until the pancetta and garlic are crisp. Try not to let the garlic brown or it will acquire a bitter flavour. Remove the pancetta and garlic with a slotted spoon and drain on kitchen paper. Leave the pancetta fat in the pan, but remove the pan from the heat.

2 Tear the rocket and radicchio leaves into a salad bowl. Sprinkle over the walnuts, pancetta and garlic. Add salt and pepper and toss to mix. Lightly crumble the Gorgonzola on top.

3 Return the frying pan to a medium heat and add the oil and vinegar. Stir until sizzling, then pour over the salad. Serve at once, to be tossed at the table.

TOMATO AND MOZZARELLA TOASTS

These resemble mini pizzas and are good with drinks before a dinner party. If you prefer, you can prepare them several hours in advance and pop them in the oven just as your guests arrive.

Preparation time 3 minutes
Cooking time 7 minutes

SERVES 6–8

3 sfilatini (thin ciabatta)
about 250ml/8 fl oz/1 cup sun-dried tomato paste
3 x 150g/5oz packets mozzarella cheese, drained and chopped
about 10ml/2 tsp dried oregano or mixed herbs
30– 45ml/2–3 tbsp olive oil
ground black pepper

1 Preheat the oven to 220ºC/ 425ºF/Gas 7. Also preheat the grill (broiler). Cut each sfilatino on the diagonal into 12–15 slices, discarding the ends. Grill (broil) until lightly toasted on both sides. Spread sun-dried tomato paste on one side of each slice of toast. Arrange the mozzarella over the tomato paste.

2 Put the toasts on baking sheets, sprinkle with herbs and pepper to taste and drizzle with oil. Bake for 5 minutes or until the mozzarella has melted and is bubbling. Leave the toasts to settle for a few minutes before serving.

Cashew Chicken

In this Chinese-inspired dish, tender pieces of chicken are stir-fried with cashew nuts, red chillies and a touch of garlic.

Preparation time 4 minutes
Cooking time 6 minutes

SERVES 4–6

450g/1lb boneless chicken
    breast portions
30ml/2 tbsp vegetable oil
2 garlic cloves, sliced
4 dried red chillies, chopped
1 red (bell) pepper, seeded and diced
30ml/2 tbsp oyster sauce
15ml/1 tbsp soy sauce
1 bunch spring onions (scallions), cut
    into 5cm/2in lengths
175g/6oz/1½ cups cashew
    nuts, roasted
coriander (cilantro) leaves, to garnish

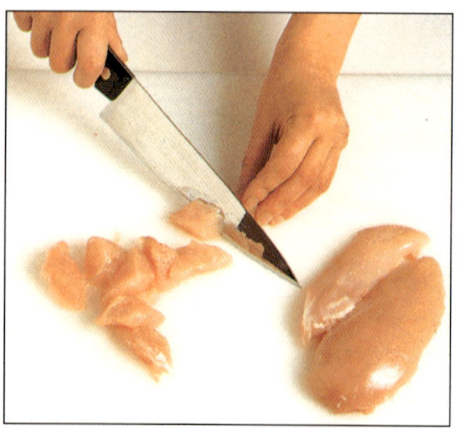

1 Remove and discard the skin from the chicken portions. With a sharp knife, cut the chicken into bite-size pieces and set aside.

2 Heat the oil in a wok and swirl it around. Add the garlic and dried chillies and fry until golden.

3 Add the chicken and stir-fry until it changes colour, then add the red pepper.

4 Stir in the oyster sauce and soy sauce. Add the spring onions and cashew nuts. Stir-fry for 1–2 minutes more. Serve garnished with a few coriander leaves.

Stir-fried Chicken with Basil and Chillies

This quick and easy chicken dish is an excellent introduction to Thai cuisine. Deep-frying the basil adds another dimension to this dish. Thai basil, which is sometimes known as Holy basil, has a unique, pungent flavour that is both spicy and sharp. The dull leaves have serrated edges.

Preparation time 3 minutes
Cooking time 7 minutes

SERVES 4–6
45ml/3 tbsp vegetable oil
4 garlic cloves, sliced
2–4 red chillies, seeded and chopped
450g/1lb chicken, cut into bite-size pieces
30–45ml/2–3 tbsp fish sauce
10ml/2 tsp dark soy sauce
5ml/1 tsp sugar
10–12 Thai basil leaves
2 red chillies, sliced, to garnish
20 Thai basil leaves, deep-fried (optional)

1 Heat the oil in a wok or large frying pan and swirl it around.

COOK'S TIP
To deep-fry Thai basil leaves, make sure that the leaves are completely dry. Deep-fry in hot oil for about 30–40 seconds, lift out using a slotted spoon and drain on kitchen paper.

2 Add the garlic and chillies and stir-fry until golden.

3 Add the chicken and stir-fry until it changes colour.

4 Season with fish sauce, soy sauce and sugar. Continue to stir-fry for 3–4 minutes or until the chicken is cooked. Stir in the fresh Thai basil leaves. Garnish with the chillies and the fried basil, if using.

Thai Chicken and Vegetable Stir-fry

Preparation time 3 minutes
Cooking time 7 minutes

SERVES 4

1 lemon grass stalk
1cm/½in piece of fresh root ginger
1 large garlic clove
30ml/2 tbsp sunflower oil
275g/10oz lean chicken, thinly sliced
½ each red and green (bell) pepper, seeded and sliced
4 spring onions (scallions), chopped
2 carrots, cut into short thin sticks
115g/4oz fine green beans
30ml/2 tbsp oyster sauce
pinch of sugar
salt and ground black pepper
crushed peanuts and coriander (cilantro) leaves, to garnish

1. Thinly slice the lemon grass. Peel and chop the ginger and garlic. Heat the oil in a frying pan over a high heat. Add the lemon grass, ginger and garlic, and stir-fry for 30 seconds until the garlic is golden and the oil is aromatic.

2. Add the chicken and stir-fry for 2 minutes. Then add the vegetables; stir-fry for 3 minutes, until the chicken is cooked and the vegetables are crisp-tender.

3. Finally, stir in the oyster sauce, sugar and seasoning to taste and stir-fry for another minute or two to mix and blend well. Serve at once, sprinkled with the peanuts and coriander leaves. Rice is the traditional accompaniment.

COOK'S TIPS
Make this quick supper dish a little hotter by adding more fresh root ginger, if you wish. If you can get hold of it, try fresh galangal instead of ginger. The flavour is similar, but has peppery overtones.

CHICKEN WITH TOMATOES AND OLIVES

Chicken breast portions or turkey, veal or pork escalopes can be flattened for quick and even cooking. They are ready-prepared in France, but are easy to do at home.

Preparation time 5 minutes
Cooking time 5 minutes

SERVES 4

4 skinless boneless chicken breast portions (150–175g/5–6oz each)
1.5ml/¼ tsp cayenne pepper
75–105ml/5–7 tbsp extra virgin olive oil
6 ripe plum tomatoes
1 garlic clove, finely chopped
16–24 stoned (pitted) black olives
small handful of fresh basil leaves
salt

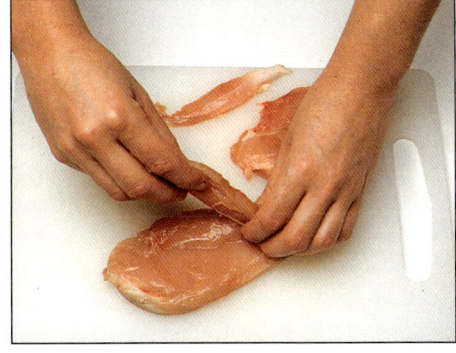

1. Carefully remove the fillets (the long finger-shaped muscle on the back of each breast) and reserve for another use.

COOK'S TIP
If the tomato skins are at all tough, remove them by cutting a cross in the base of each tomato with a knife, then plunging them into boiling water for about 45 seconds. The skin should simply peel off. If you have a gas stove, you can achieve the same result by preparing the tomatoes in the same way, spearing each one in turn on a fork and rotating it in the open flame until the skin peels back.

2. Place each chicken breast portions between two sheets of greaseproof (waxed) paper or clear film (plastic wrap) and pound with the flat side of a meat hammer or roll out with a rolling pin to flatten to about 1cm/½in thick. Season with the cayenne pepper.

3. Heat 45–60ml/3–4 tbsp of the olive oil in a large heavy frying pan over a medium-high heat. Add the flattened chicken breasts and cook for 3–4 minutes until golden brown and just cooked, turning them once. Transfer the chicken to warmed serving plates and season with a little salt. Keep the chicken hot.

4. Peel the tomatoes (see Cook's Tip), then seed and chop.

5. Wipe out the frying pan and return to the heat. Add another 30–45ml/2–3 tbsp of olive oil and fry the garlic for 1 minute until golden and fragrant. Stir in the olives, cook for a further 1 minute, then stir in the tomatoes. Shred the basil leaves and stir into the olive and tomato mixture, then spoon it over the chicken and serve immediately.

CRUMBED TURKEY WITH CAPERS

A staple of bistro cooking, these thin slices of poultry or meat, called escalopes or sometimes paillards, cook very quickly and can be served with all kinds of sauces.

Preparation time 6 minutes
Cooking time 4 minutes

SERVES 2

4 thin turkey breast escalopes (US scallops), (about 75g/3oz each)
1 large unwaxed lemon
2.5ml/ ½ tsp chopped fresh sage
60–75ml/4–5 tbsp extra virgin olive oil
50g/2oz/ ½ cup fine dry breadcrumbs
15ml/1 tbsp capers, rinsed and drained
salt and ground black pepper
sage leaves and lemon wedges, to garnish

1 Place the turkey escalopes between two sheets of greaseproof (waxed) paper or clear film (plastic wrap) and pound with the flat side of a meat hammer or roll with a rolling pin to flatten to about a 5mm/¼ in thickness.

2 With a vegetable peeler, remove four pieces of lemon rind. Cut them into thin julienne strips, cover with clear film and set aside. Grate the remainder of the lemon rind and squeeze the lemon. Put the grated rind in a large shallow dish and add the sage, salt and pepper. Stir in 15ml/1 tbsp of the lemon juice, reserving the rest, and about 15ml/1 tbsp of the olive oil, then add the turkey, turn to coat and set aside.

3 Place the breadcrumbs in another shallow dish and dip the escalopes in the crumbs, coating both sides evenly. In a heavy frying pan heat 30ml/2 tbsp of the olive oil over a high heat, add the escalopes and cook for 2–3 minutes, turning once, until golden. Transfer to two warmed plates and keep warm.

4 Wipe out the pan, add the remaining oil, the lemon julienne and the capers and heat through, stirring constantly. Spoon a little sauce over the turkey and garnish with sage leaves and lemon.

Veal with Lemon and Vermouth

Popular in Italian restaurants, this dish is very easy to make at home.

Preparation time 4 minutes
Cooking time 4 minutes

SERVES 4

4 veal escalopes (US scallops)
30–45 ml/2–3 tbsp plain (all-purpose) flour
50g/2oz/¼ cup butter
60ml/4 tbsp olive oil
60ml/4 tbsp dry white vermouth
45ml/3 tbsp lemon juice
salt and ground black pepper
lemon rind, lemon wedges and fresh parsley, to garnish
green beans and peperonata, to serve

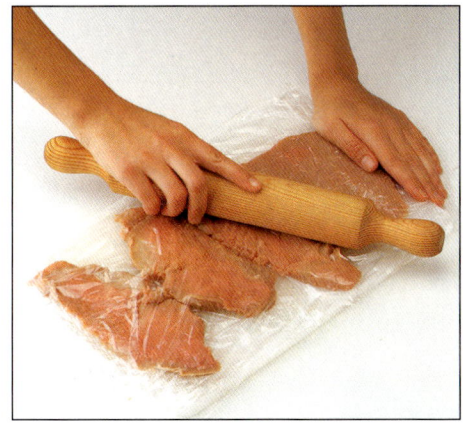

1. Put each escalope between two sheets of greaseproof (waxed) paper or clear film (plastic wrap) and pound until thin. Cut the pounded escalopes in half or quarters, and coat in the flour, seasoned with salt and ground black pepper.

COOK'S TIP
To make the peperonata suggested as an accompaniment, heat 75ml/5 tbsp olive oil in a pan, add 1 chopped onion, 2 diced red (bell) peppers, 1 crushed garlic clove and 2 chopped tomatoes and cook gently for about 15 minutes. Serve hot or cold.

2. Melt the butter with half the oil in a large, heavy frying pan until sizzling. Add as many escalopes (scallops) as the pan will hold. Fry over a medium to high heat for 1–2 minutes on each side until lightly coloured. Remove with a fish slice (spatula) and keep hot. Add the remaining oil and cook the remaining veal in the same way.

3. Remove the pan from the heat and add the vermouth and the lemon juice. Stir vigorously to mix with the pan juices, then return the pan to the heat and return all the veal to the pan. Spoon the sauce over the escalopes. Gently shake the pan over a medium heat until all of the escalopes are coated in the sauce and heated through.

4. Serve immediately, garnished with lemon rind, lemon wedges and parsley. Lightly cooked green beans and peperonata make a delicious accompaniment.

VARIATION
Use skinless boneless chicken breasts portions instead of the veal. If thick, cut them in half before pounding.

Pan-Fried Veal Chops

Veal chops from the loin are an expensive cut and are best cooked quickly and simply. The flavour of basil goes well with veal, but you could use another herb, such as rosemary or parsley.

Preparation time 2 minutes
Cooking time 7–8 minutes

SERVES 2
25g/1oz/2 tbsp butter, softened
15ml/1 tbsp Dijon mustard
15ml/1 tbsp chopped fresh basil
olive oil, for brushing
2 veal loin chops, 2.5cm/1in thick (about 225g/8oz each)
ground black pepper
fresh basil sprigs, to garnish

1 To make the basil butter, cream the butter with the mustard and chopped basil in a small bowl, then season with pepper.

2 Lightly oil a heavy frying pan or griddle. Set over a high heat until very hot but not smoking. Brush both sides of each chop with a little oil and season with a little pepper.

3 Place the chops on the pan or griddle and reduce the heat to medium. Cook for 4–5 minutes, turn and cook for 3–4 minutes more until done as preferred (medium-rare meat will still be slightly soft when pressed, medium meat will be springy and well-done firm). Top each chop with half the basil butter and serve, garnished with basil.

Veal with Tarragon Sauce

These thin slices of veal need little cooking, and the sauce is made very quickly as well.

Preparation time 4 minutes
Cooking time 6 minutes

SERVES 4
4 veal escalopes (US scallops) (about 115–150g/4–5oz each)
15g/½oz/1 tbsp butter
30ml/2 tbsp brandy
250ml/8fl oz/1 cup chicken or beef stock
15ml/1 tbsp chopped fresh tarragon
salt and ground black pepper
fresh tarragon sprigs, to garnish

1 Place the veal slices between two sheets of greaseproof (waxed) paper or clear film (plastic wrap) and pound with the flat side of a meat mallet or roll them with a rolling pin to flatten to about 5mm/¼in thickness. Season with salt and ground black pepper.

2 Melt the butter in a large frying pan over a medium-high heat. Add enough meat to the pan to fit easily in one layer (do not overcrowd the pan, cook in batches if necessary) and cook for 1½–2 minutes, turning once. Each escalope should be lightly browned, but must not be overcooked. Transfer to a platter and cover to keep warm.

3 Add the brandy to the pan, then pour in the stock and bring to the boil. Add the tarragon and continue boiling until the liquid is reduced by half.

4 Return the veal to the pan with any accumulated juices and heat through. Serve immediately, garnished with tarragon sprigs.

Calf's Liver with Honey

Liver is the perfect choice for a quick meal. Although it can be braised, it is at its best when simply flashed in a hot pan. Cook the liver until it is browned on the outside but still rosy pink in the centre.

Preparation time 2 minutes
Cooking time 4–5 minutes

SERVES 4

4 slices calf's liver (about 175g/6oz each and 1cm/½in thick)
plain (all-purpose) flour, for dusting
25g/1oz/2 tbsp butter
30ml/2 tbsp vegetable oil
30ml/2 tbsp sherry vinegar or red wine vinegar
30–45ml/2–3 tbsp chicken stock
15ml/1 tbsp clear honey
salt and ground black pepper
watercress sprigs, to garnish

1 Wipe the liver slices with damp kitchen paper, then season both sides with a little salt and pepper and dust the slices lightly with flour, shaking off any excess.

COOK'S TIP
It is important to use calf's liver, as it is tender and delicately flavoured. You could get away with lamb's liver, but don't use any other type.

2 In a large heavy frying pan, melt half of the butter with the oil over a high heat and swirl to blend thoroughly.

3 Add the liver slices to the pan and cook for 1–2 minutes until browned on one side, then turn and cook for a further 1 minute. Transfer to warmed plates and keep warm.

4 Stir the vinegar, stock and honey into the pan. Boil for about 1 minute, stirring constantly, then add the remaining butter, stirring until melted and smooth. Spoon over the liver slices and garnish with watercress sprigs.

PORK IN SWEET-AND-SOUR SAUCE

The combination of sweet-and-sour flavours is popular in Venetian cooking, especially with meat and liver. This delicious recipe is given extra bite with the addition of crushed mixed peppercorns.

Preparation time 2–3 minutes
Cooking time 6 minutes

SERVES 2

1 whole pork fillet (tenderloin), about 350g/12oz
25ml/1½ tbsp plain (all-purpose) flour
30–45ml/2–3 tbsp olive oil
250ml/8fl oz/1 cup dry white wine
30ml/2 tbsp white wine vinegar
10ml/2 tsp granulated sugar
15ml/1 tbsp mixed peppercorns, coarsely ground
salt and ground black pepper
cooked broad (fava) beans tossed with grilled (broiled) bacon, to serve

1 Cut the pork diagonally into thin slices. Place between two sheets of clear film (plastic wrap) and pound lightly with a rolling pin.

2 Spread out the flour in a shallow bowl. Season well and coat the meat. Alternatively, put the seasoned flour in a strong plastic bag, add the pork and shake to coat.

3 Heat 15ml/1 tbsp of the oil in a wide heavy pan or frying pan and add as many slices of pork as the pan will hold. Fry over a medium to high heat for 2–3 minutes on each side until crisp and tender. Remove with a fish slice (spatula). Repeat with the remaining pork, adding more oil as necessary.

4 Mix the wine, vinegar and sugar in a jug (pitcher). Pour into the pan and stir over a high heat until reduced. Stir in the peppercorns and return the pork to the pan. Spoon the sauce over the pork until it is evenly coated and heated through. Serve with cooked broad beans tossed with grilled bacon.

Pork with Camembert

When it comes to speedy feasts, pork fillet is an excellent choice. Beautifully tender, it needs little cooking and is delicious served with a creamy cheese sauce.

Preparation time 2 minutes
Cooking time 7–8 minutes

SERVES 4

450g/1lb pork fillet (tenderloin)
15g/½oz/1 tbsp butter
45ml/3 tbsp sparkling dry (hard) cider or dry white wine
120–175ml/4–6fl oz/½–¾ cup crème fraîche or whipping cream
15ml/1 tbsp chopped fresh mixed herbs, such as marjoram, thyme and sage
½ Camembert cheese (115g/4oz), rind removed (65g/2½oz without rind), sliced
7.5ml/1½ tsp Dijon mustard
ground black pepper
fresh parsley, to garnish

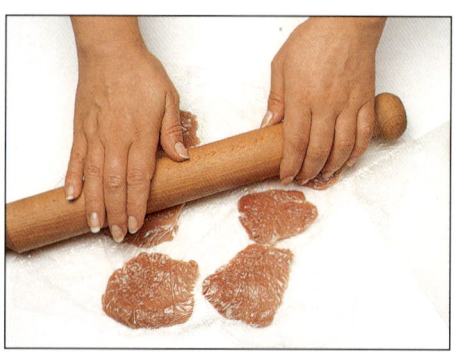

1 Slice the pork fillet crossways into small steaks about 2cm/¾in thick. Place between two sheets of greaseproof (waxed) paper or clear film (plastic wrap) and pound with the flat side of a meat mallet or roll with a rolling pin to flatten to a thickness of 1cm/½in. Sprinkle with pepper.

VARIATION
Any creamy cheese that is not too soft can be used instead of Camembert. Try Cambazola or Brie for a change.

2 Melt the butter in a heavy frying pan over a medium-high heat until it begins to brown, then add the meat. Cook for 5 minutes, turning once, or until just cooked through and the meat is springy when pressed. Transfer to a warmed dish and cover to keep warm.

3 Add the cider or wine and bring to the boil, scraping the bottom of the pan. Stir in the cream and herbs and bring back to the boil.

4 Add the cheese and mustard and any accumulated juices from the meat. Stir until the cheese melts. Add a little more cream if needed and adjust the seasoning. Serve the pork with the sauce and garnish with parsley.

Salmon with Green Peppercorns

A fashionable discovery of nouvelle cuisine, green peppercorns add piquancy to all kinds of sauces and stews. Available pickled in jars or cans, they are great to keep on hand in your store cupboard.

Preparation time 1 minute
Cooking time 9 minutes

SERVES 4

15g/ ½ oz/1 tbsp butter
2 or 3 shallots, finely chopped
15ml/1 tbsp brandy (optional)
60ml/4 tbsp dry white wine
90ml/6 tbsp fish or chicken stock
120ml/4fl oz/ ½ cup whipping cream
30–45ml/2–3 tbsp green peppercorns in brine, rinsed and drained
15–30ml/1–2 tbsp vegetable oil
4 pieces salmon fillet (175–200g/ 6–7oz each)
salt and ground black pepper
fresh parsley, to garnish

1 Melt the butter in a heavy pan over a medium heat. Add the shallots and cook for 1 minute until just softened.

2 Add the brandy, if using, and the white wine. Stir well, then pour in the stock and bring to the boil. Continue to boil hard until the liquid has reduced by three-quarters, stirring occasionally.

3 Reduce the heat, then add the cream and half the green peppercorns, crushing them slightly with the back of a spoon. Cook very gently for 4 minutes until the sauce is slightly thickened, then strain and stir in the remaining peppercorns. Keep the sauce warm over a very low heat, stirring occasionally, while you cook the salmon.

4 In a large heavy frying pan, heat the oil over a medium-high heat until very hot. Lightly season the salmon and cook for 3–4 minutes or until the flesh is opaque and flakes easily when tested with the tip of a sharp knife. Arrange the fish on warmed plates and pour over the sauce. Garnish with parsley.

Halibut with Tomato Vinaigrette

Sauce vièrge, a lightly cooked mixture of tomatoes, aromatic fresh herbs and olive oil, can either be served at room temperature or, as in this dish, slightly warm.

Preparation time 4 minutes
Cooking time 5–6 minutes

SERVES 2

3 large ripe beefsteak tomatoes, peeled, seeded and chopped
2 shallots or 1 small red onion, finely chopped
1 garlic clove, crushed
90ml/6 tbsp chopped mixed fresh herbs, such as parsley, coriander (cilantro), basil, chervil or chives
120ml/4fl oz/ ½ cup extra virgin olive oil, plus extra for greasing
4 halibut fillets or steaks (175–200g/6–7oz each)
salt and ground black pepper
green salad, to serve

1 In a small pan, mix together the tomatoes, shallots or onion, garlic and herbs. Stir in the oil and season with salt and ground black pepper. Cover the pan and leave the sauce to stand at room temperature while you grill (broil) the fish.

COOK'S TIP
If time permits, leave the sauce to stand for up to an hour.

2 Preheat the grill (broiler). Line a grill pan with foil and brush the foil lightly with oil.

3 Season the fish with salt and pepper. Place the fish on the foil and brush with a little oil. Grill for 5–6 minutes until the flesh is opaque and the top browned.

4 Meanwhile, heat the sauce gently for a few minutes. Serve the fish with the sauce and a salad.

Pan-Fried Sole with Lemon Butter Sauce

The delicate flavour and texture of sole is brought out in this simple, classic recipe. Lemon sole is used here because it is often easier to obtain than Dover sole.

Preparation time 1 minute
Cooking time 9 minutes

SERVES 2

30–45ml/2–3 tbsp plain (all-purpose) flour
4 lemon sole fillets
45ml/3 tbsp olive oil
50g/2oz/¼ cup butter
60ml/4 tbsp lemon juice
30ml/2 tbsp rinsed bottled capers
salt and ground black pepper
fresh flat leaf parsley and lemon wedges, to garnish

1 Season the flour with salt and black pepper. Coat the sole fillets evenly on both sides. Heat the oil with half the butter in a large shallow pan until foaming. Add two sole fillets and fry over a medium heat for 2–3 minutes on each side.

2 Lift out the sole fillets with a fish slice (spatula) and place on a warmed serving platter. Keep hot. Fry the remaining sole fillets in the same way, then lift them out carefully and add them to the platter.

3 Remove the pan from the heat and add the lemon juice and remaining butter. Return the pan to a high heat and stir vigorously until the pan juices are sizzling and beginning to turn golden brown. Remove from the heat and stir in the capers.

4 Pour the pan juices over the sole, sprinkle with salt and pepper to taste and garnish with the parsley. Add the lemon wedges and serve immediately.

COOK'S TIPS

It is important to cook the pan juices to the right colour after removing the fish. Too pale, and they will taste insipid, too dark, and they may taste bitter. Take great care not to be distracted at this point so that you can watch the colour of the juices change to a golden brown. If you don't like the flavour of capers, leave them out since the butter sauce is quite good enough to serve on its own.

Prawn and Vegetable Balti

A delicious accompaniment to other Balti dishes. Double the quantities if serving it solo.

Preparation time 3 minutes
Cooking time 7 minutes

SERVES 4

175g/6oz cooked, peeled prawns (shrimp), thawed if frozen
30ml/2 tbsp corn oil
1.5ml/¼ tsp onion seeds
4–6 curry leaves
115g/4oz/1 cup frozen peas
115g/4oz/⅔ cup frozen sweetcorn
1 large courgette (zucchini), sliced
1 red (bell) pepper, seeded and roughly diced
5ml/1 tsp crushed coriander seeds
5ml/1 tsp crushed dried red chillies
15ml/1 tbsp lemon juice
salt
15ml/1 tbsp fresh coriander (cilantro) leaves, to garnish

1 Drain any excess liquid from the prawns and pat them dry on kitchen paper. Heat the oil with the onion seeds and curry leaves in a non-stick wok or heavy frying pan.

Cook's Tip
The best way to crush whole seeds is to use an electric spice grinder, coffee grinder reserved for this purpose or a small marble pestle and mortar.

2 Add the prawns to the wok or frying pan and stir-fry until any liquid has evaporated.

3 Add the peas, sweetcorn, courgette and pepper and stir-fry for 3–5 minutes.

4 Add the coriander seeds, dried red chillies and lemon juice. Toss over the heat for 1 minute, season to taste with salt and serve immediately, garnished with the fresh coriander leaves.

GREEN PRAWN CURRY

A popular fragrant creamy curry that takes very little time to prepare. It can also be made with thin strips of chicken.

Preparation time 2 minutes
Cooking time 8 minutes

SERVES 4–6

30ml/2 tbsp vegetable oil
30ml/2 tbsp green curry paste
450g/1lb raw king prawns (jumbo shrimp), shelled and deveined
4 kaffir lime leaves, torn
1 lemon grass stalk, bruised and chopped
250ml/8fl oz/1 cup coconut milk
30ml/2 tbsp fish sauce
½ cucumber, seeded and cut into thin batons
10–15 fresh basil leaves
sliced green chillies, to garnish

1 Heat the oil in a frying pan. Add the green curry paste and fry until bubbling and fragrant.

2 Add the prawns, lime leaves and lemon grass. Fry for 2 minutes, until the prawns are pink.

3 Stir in the coconut milk and bring to a gentle boil. Simmer, stirring, for about 5 minutes or until the prawns are tender.

4 Stir in the fish sauce and cucumber. Tear the basil leaves and add them too, then top with the green chillies and serve.

SAUTÉED SCALLOPS

Scallops go well with all sorts of sauces, but simple cooking is the best way to enjoy their delicate, fresh-from-the-sea flavour.

Preparation time 1 minute
Cooking time 5 minutes

SERVES 2

450g/1lb shelled scallops
25g/1oz/2 tbsp butter
30ml/2 tbsp dry white vermouth
15ml/1 tbsp finely chopped
    fresh parsley
salt and ground black pepper

1 Rinse the scallops under cold running water to remove any sand or grit. Drain them well and pat dry using kitchen paper. Spread them out and season them lightly with salt and pepper.

2 In a frying pan large enough to hold the scallops in one layer, heat half the butter until it begins to colour. Sauté the scallops for 3–5 minutes, turning, until golden brown on both sides and just firm to the touch. Remove to a serving platter and cover to keep hot.

3 Add the vermouth to the hot frying pan, swirl in the remaining butter, stir in the parsley and pour the sauce over the scallops. Serve immediately.

GARLICKY SCALLOPS AND PRAWNS

Scallops and prawns provide a healthy meal in next to no time. This method of cooking comes from Provence in France.

Preparation time 1 minute
Cooking time 4–5 minutes

SERVES 2–4

6 large shelled scallops
6–8 large raw prawns
    (shrimp), peeled
plain (all-purpose) flour, for dusting
30–45ml/2–3 tbsp olive oil
1 garlic clove, finely chopped
15ml/1 tbsp chopped fresh basil
30–45ml/2–3 tbsp lemon juice
salt and ground black pepper

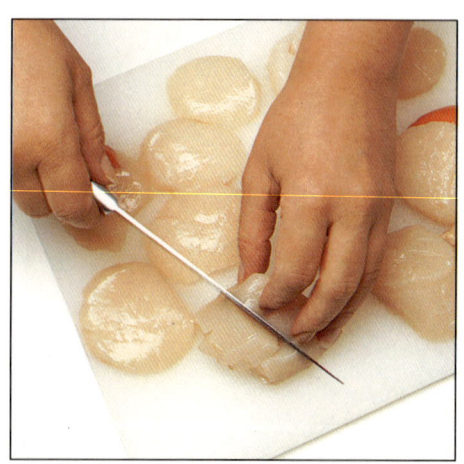 

1 Rinse the scallops under cold running water to remove any sand or grit. Drain, then pat dry using kitchen paper. Cut them in half crossways. Season the scallops and prawns with salt and pepper and dust lightly with flour. Heat the olive oil in a large frying pan over a high heat and add the scallops and prawns.

2 Reduce the heat slightly and cook for 2 minutes, then turn the scallops and prawns and add the garlic and basil, shaking the pan to distribute them evenly. Cook for a further 2 minutes until the scallops are golden and just firm to the touch. Sprinkle over the lemon juice and toss well to blend. Serve immediately.

Spaghetti with Rocket Pesto

This is the pesto for real rocket lovers. It is sharp and peppery, and delicious for a summer meal with a glass of chilled wine.

Preparation time 4 minutes
Cooking time 6 minutes

SERVES 4

4 garlic cloves
90ml/6 tbsp pine nuts
2 large handfuls rocket (arugula), total weight about 150g/5oz, stalks removed
50g/2oz/⅔ cup freshly grated Parmesan cheese
50g/2oz/⅔ cup freshly grated Pecorino cheese
90ml/6 tbsp extra virgin olive oil
400g/14oz fresh or dried spaghetti
salt and ground black pepper
freshly grated Parmesan and Pecorino cheese, to serve

1 Put the garlic and pine nuts in a blender or food processor and process until finely chopped.

2 Add the rocket, Parmesan and Pecorino, oil and salt and pepper to taste and process for about 5 seconds. Stop and scrape down the side of the bowl. Process for 5–10 seconds more until a smooth paste is formed.

3 Cook the spaghetti in a pan of salted boiling water according to the packet instructions.

4 Turn the pesto into a large bowl. Just before the pasta is ready, add 1–2 ladlefuls of the cooking water to the pesto and stir well to mix.

5 Drain the pasta, tip it into the bowl of pesto and toss well to mix. Serve immediately, with the grated cheeses handed separately.

VARIATION
To temper the flavour of the rocket and make the pesto milder, add 115g/4oz/½ cup mascarpone or ricotta cheese to the pesto in step 4 and mix well before adding the water.

CONCHIGLIE FROM PISA

Nothing could be simpler — or more refreshing — than hot pasta tossed with fresh ripe tomatoes, ricotta and sweet basil.

Preparation time 4 minutes
Cooking time 6 minutes

SERVES 6

350g/12oz/3 cups dried conchiglie
125g/4½oz/generous ½ cup
   ricotta cheese
6 ripe Italian plum tomatoes, diced
2 garlic cloves, crushed
1 handful fresh basil leaves, shredded,
   plus extra basil leaves to garnish
60ml/4 tbsp extra virgin olive oil
salt and ground black pepper

1. Cook the pasta in lightly salted boiling water according to the instructions on the packet.

2. Meanwhile, put the ricotta in a small mixing bowl and mash with a fork.

VARIATIONS

You can use diced mozzarella instead of ricotta cheese and call the dish Conchiglie Caprese, after the salad of tomatoes, mozzarella and basil known as Caprese.

An avocado is the ideal ingredient for adding extra colour and flavour to this pasta dish. Halve, stone (pit) and peel, then dice the flesh. Toss it with the hot pasta at the last minute.

3. Add the tomatoes, garlic and basil, with salt and pepper to taste, and mix well. Add the olive oil and whisk thoroughly. Taste for seasoning and adjust, if necessary.

4. Drain the cooked pasta, tip it into the ricotta mixture and toss well to mix. Garnish with basil leaves and serve immediately.

Noodles with Pineapple, Ginger and Chillies

Preparation and cooking time 8–10 minutes

SERVES 4

275g/10oz dried noodles
4 fresh or drained, canned pineapple rings
45ml/3 tbsp soft light brown sugar
60ml/4 tbsp fresh lime juice
60ml/4 tbsp coconut milk
30ml/2 tbsp fish sauce
30ml/2 tbsp grated fresh root ginger
2 garlic cloves, finely chopped
1 ripe mango or 2 peaches, finely diced

FOR THE GARNISH
2 spring onions (scallions), sliced
2 fresh red chillies, shredded
fresh mint leaves

[1] Cook the noodles in a large pan of boiling water until tender, following the directions on the packet.

[2] Meanwhile, place the pineapple rings on a flameproof dish, sprinkle with 30ml/2 tbsp of the sugar and grill (broil) until golden. Cut into small dice.

[3] Mix the lime juice, coconut milk and fish sauce in a salad bowl. Add the remaining brown sugar, with the ginger and garlic, and whisk well. Drain the noodles, refresh under cold water and drain again. Add to the bowl with the noodles and pineapple.

[4] Add the mango or peaches and toss lightly. Scatter the spring onions, chillies and mint over. Serve.

Buckwheat Noodles with Smoked Salmon

Young pea sprouts are only available for a short time. You can substitute salad cress, rocket, young leeks or your favourite green vegetable or herb in this dish.

Preparation and cooking time 8–10 minutes

SERVES 4

225g/8oz buckwheat or soba noodles
15ml/1 tbsp oyster sauce
juice of ½ lemon
30–45ml/2–3 tbsp light olive oil
115g/4oz smoked salmon, cut into fine strips
115g/4oz young pea sprouts
2 ripe tomatoes, peeled, seeded and cut into strips
15ml/1 tbsp chopped chives
salt and ground black pepper

[1] Cook the buckwheat or soba noodles in a large saucepan of boiling water, following the directions on the packet. Drain, then tip into a colander and rinse under cold running water. Drain well, shaking the colander to extract any remaining water.

[2] Tip the noodles into a large bowl. Add the oyster sauce and lemon juice and season with pepper to taste. Moisten with the olive oil.

[3] Add the smoked salmon, pea sprouts, tomatoes and chives. Mix well and serve immediately.

Tagliatelle with Prosciutto and Asparagus

A stunning dish, this is very easy to make. Serve it for a special occasion.

Preparation and cooking time 7–10 minutes

SERVES 4

350g/12oz fresh or dried tagliatelle
25g/1oz/2 tbsp butter
15ml/1 tbsp olive oil
225g/8oz asparagus tips
1 garlic clove, chopped
115g/4oz prosciutto, sliced into strips
30ml/2 tbsp chopped fresh sage
150ml/¼ pint/⅔ cup single (light) cream
115g/4oz/1 cup grated Double Gloucester cheese
115g/4oz/1 cup grated Gruyère cheese
fresh sage leaves, to garnish

1 Cook the tagliatelle in a large pan of boiling water until tender, following the instructions on the packet.

2 Meanwhile, melt the butter and oil in a frying pan and gently fry the asparagus tips for 3–4 minutes, or until almost tender.

3 Stir in the garlic and prosciutto and fry for 1 minute.

4 Stir in the sage leaves and fry for a further 1 minute, then pour in the cream. Bring to the boil over a medium heat, stirring frequently.

5 Tip in the grated Double Gloucester and Gruyère cheeses. Simmer gently, stirring occasionally until thoroughly melted. Season to taste. Drain the pasta thoroughly and tip it into a bowl. Add the sauce and toss to coat. Serve immediately, garnished with fresh sage.

RAVIOLI WITH FOUR-CHEESE SAUCE

This has a smooth cheese sauce that coats the pasta very evenly.

Preparation and cooking time 5–6 minutes

SERVES 4

350g/12oz fresh ravioli
50g/2oz/¼ cup butter
50g/2oz/½ cup plain (all-purpose) flour
450ml/¾ pint/scant 2 cups milk
50g/2oz Parmesan cheese
50g/2oz Edam cheese
50g/2oz Gruyère cheese
50g/2oz Fontina cheese
salt and ground black pepper
fresh flat leaf parsley, to garnish

1. Cook the pasta following the instructions on the packet.

2. Meanwhile, melt the butter in a pan, stir in the flour and cook for 2 minutes, stirring.

3. Gradually stir in the milk until well blended.

4. Bring the milk to the boil over a low heat, stirring constantly until thickened.

5. Grate the cheeses and stir them into the sauce. Stir until they are just beginning to melt. Remove the sauce from the heat and season with salt and pepper.

6. Drain the pasta thoroughly and turn it into a large serving bowl. Pour over the sauce and toss to coat. Serve immediately, garnished with the fresh parsley.

COOK'S TIP

If you cannot find all of the above cheeses, simply substitute your own. What is essential is to have a total quantity of 225g/8oz/2 cups grated cheese and to include Parmesan in the selection. Buy Parmesan in one piece and grate it yourself – using the ready-grated cheese may save time, but the flavour will not be so good.

Spaghetti Alla Carbonara

This is a classic pasta dish. If you use fresh spaghetti, cook it at the last minute as it takes very little time.

Preparation and cooking time 7–10 minutes

SERVES 4

350g/12oz spaghetti
15ml/1 tbsp olive oil
1 onion, chopped
115g/4oz streaky (fatty) bacon or pancetta, rind removed and diced
1 garlic clove, chopped
3 eggs
300ml/ ½ pint/1¼ cups double (heavy) cream
50g/2oz Parmesan cheese
salt and ground black pepper
chopped fresh basil, to garnish

1 Cook the pasta following the instructions on the packet.

2 Meanwhile, heat the oil in a frying pan and fry the onion and bacon or pancetta for 5 minutes until softened. Stir in the garlic and fry for a further 2 minutes, stirring.

3 Meanwhile, beat the eggs in a bowl, then stir in the cream and season with salt and pepper. Grate the Parmesan cheese and stir it into the cream mixture.

4 Stir the cream mixture into the onion and bacon and cook over a low heat for a few minutes, stirring constantly until heated through. Season to taste.

5 Drain the pasta thoroughly and turn it into a large serving bowl. Pour over the sauce and toss to coat. Serve immediately, garnished with chopped fresh basil.

Cook's Tips
Italians would use pancetta that is lightly cured but similar to streaky bacon. You can buy it in most supermarkets and delicatessens. If you use bacon, look out for packs of chopped bacon – a real time-saver.

Spinach Tagliarini with Asparagus

Fresh pasta is a boon to the busy cook. You may not be able to locate spinach tagliarini, but any fresh pasta will work just as well.

Preparation time 2–4 minutes
Cooking time 6–8 minutes

SERVES 4–6
2 skinless, boneless chicken
 breast portions
15ml/1 tbsp light soy sauce
30ml/2 tbsp sherry
30ml/2 tbsp cornflour (cornstarch)
8 spring onions (scallions), cut into
 2.5cm/1in diagonal slices
1–2 garlic cloves, crushed
needle shreds of rind of ½ lemon
150ml/¼ pint/⅔ cup chicken stock
5ml/1 tsp caster (superfine) sugar
30ml/2 tbsp lemon juice
225g/8oz slender asparagus spears,
 cut in 7.5cm/3in lengths
450g/1lb fresh spinach tagliarini
salt and ground black pepper

1 Place the chicken breast portions between two sheets of clear film (plastic wrap) and flatten to a thickness of 5mm/¼in with a rolling-pin. Cut the chicken into 2.5cm/1in strips across the grain. Put the chicken into a bowl with the soy sauce, sherry, cornflour and seasoning. Toss to coat.

COOK'S TIP
Fresh pasta is ready as soon as it rises to the surface of the boiling water.

2 In a large non-stick frying pan, put the chicken, spring onions, garlic and needle shreds of lemon rind. Add the chicken stock and bring to the boil, stirring constantly until thickened. Add the sugar, lemon juice and asparagus. Simmer for 4–5 minutes until tender.

3 Meanwhile, cook the pasta in a large pan of boiling salted water for 2–3 minutes until just tender. Drain thoroughly. Arrange on serving plates and spoon over the chicken and asparagus sauce. Serve the dish immediately.

French Goat's Cheese Salad

Preparation time 2–3 minutes
Cooking time 6 minutes

SERVES 4

200g/7oz bag prepared mixed salad leaves
4 rashers (strips) back (lean) bacon
115g/4oz full fat goat's cheese
16 thin slices French bread

FOR THE DRESSING
60ml/4 tbsp olive oil
15ml/1 tbsp tarragon vinegar
10ml/2 tsp walnut oil
5ml/1 tsp Dijon mustard
5ml/1 tsp wholegrain mustard
salt and ground black pepper

1. Preheat the grill (broiler) to medium. Rinse and dry the salad leaves, then arrange in four bowls. Place the ingredients for the dressing in a screw-topped jar, shake together well and reserve.

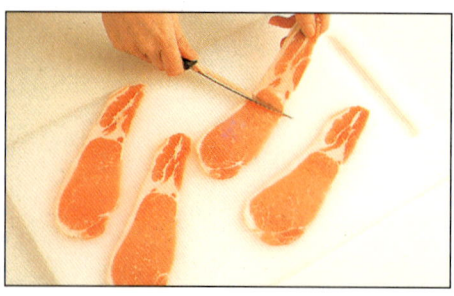

2. Lay the bacon rashers on a board, then stretch with the back of a knife and cut each into four. Roll each piece up and grill (broil) for about 2–3 minutes.

3. Meanwhile, slice the goat's cheese into eight and halve each slice. Top each slice of bread with a piece of goat's cheese and place under the grill. Turn over the bacon and continue cooking with the goat's cheese toasts until the cheese is golden and bubbling.

4. Arrange the bacon rolls and toasts on top of the prepared salad leaves. Shake the dressing well and pour a little of the dressing over each salad. Serve at once.

VARIATION
If you prefer, just slice the goat's cheese and place on toasted French bread. Or use wholemeal (wholewheat) toast for a nutty flavour.

Greek Salad Pittas

Horiatiki is the Greek name for this classic salad made with feta – a sheep's milk cheese. It is great with pitta bread.

Preparation time 5 minutes
Cooking time 2 minutes

MAKES 4

115g/4oz/1 cup diced feta cheese
¼ cucumber, peeled and diced
8 cherry tomatoes, quartered
½ small green (bell) pepper, seeded and thinly sliced
¼ small onion, thinly sliced
8 black olives, stoned (pitted) and halved
30ml/2 tbsp olive oil
5ml/1 tsp dried oregano
4 large pitta breads
60ml/4 tbsp natural (plain) yogurt
5ml/1 tsp dried mint
salt and ground black pepper
fresh mint, to garnish

1. Place the cheese, cucumber, tomatoes, pepper, onion and olives in a bowl. Stir in the olive oil and oregano, season and set aside.

2. Place the pitta breads in a toaster or under a preheated grill (broiler) for about 2 minutes, until puffed up. Meanwhile, to make the dressing, mix the yogurt with the dried mint, season well and reserve.

3. Holding the hot pittas in a dish towel, slice each one down one of the longer sides and open out to form a pocket.

4. Divide the prepared salad among the pitta bread pockets and drizzle over a spoonful of the yogurt dressing. Serve the filled pittas immediately, garnished with fresh mint. Offer the remaining dressing separately.

Spinach Salad with Bacon and Prawns

Preparation time 4 minutes
Cooking time 6 minutes

Serves 4

105ml/7 tbsp olive oil
30ml/2 tbsp sherry vinegar
2 garlic cloves, finely chopped
5ml/1 tsp Dijon mustard
12 cooked king prawns
 (jumbo shrimp)
115g/4oz rindless streaky (fatty)
 bacon, cut into strips
about 115g/4oz fresh young
 spinach leaves
½ head oakleaf lettuce, roughly torn
salt and ground black pepper

1. To make the dressing, whisk together 90ml/6 tbsp of the olive oil with the vinegar, garlic, mustard and seasoning in a small pan. Heat gently until thickened slightly, then keep warm.

2. Carefully peel the prawns, leaving the tails intact.

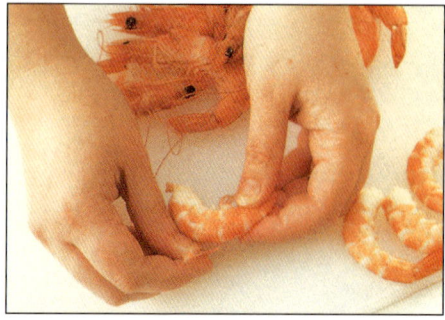

3. Heat the remaining oil in a frying pan and fry the bacon until crisp, stirring occasionally. Add the prawns and stir-fry until evenly warmed through.

4. Trim the spinach leaves and arrange them with the torn oakleaf lettuce leaves on four individual serving plates.

5. Spoon the bacon and prawns on to the salad leaves, then pour over the hot dressing. Serve immediately.

Cook's Tip
Sherry vinegar lends its pungent flavour to this delicious salad. You can buy it from large supermarkets and good delicatessens.

CAESAR SALAD

This famous salad was created in the 1920s by a Tijuanan chef called Caesar Cardini.

Preparation time 2 minutes
Cooking time 6–8 minutes

SERVES 4

1 large cos (romaine) lettuce or other crisp lettuce
4 thick slices white or Granary (whole-wheat) bread, crusts removed, cubed
45ml/3 tbsp olive oil
1 garlic clove, crushed
25g/1oz/⅓ cup freshly grated Parmesan cheese

FOR THE DRESSING
1 egg
1 garlic clove, chopped
30ml/2 tbsp lemon juice
dash of Worcestershire sauce
3 anchovy fillets, chopped
120ml/4fl oz/½ cup olive oil
salt and ground black pepper

1 Preheat the oven to 220°C/425°F/Gas 7. Separate, rinse and dry the lettuce leaves. Roughly tear the outer leaves of the lettuce and chop the heart.

2 Arrange the lettuce in a salad bowl. Mix together the cubed bread, olive oil and garlic in a separate bowl. Leave for 2 minutes, until the bread has soaked up the flavoured oil. Lay the bread cubes on a baking sheet and place in the oven for about 6–8 minutes (keeping an eye on them) until golden brown.

3 Meanwhile, make the dressing. Break the egg into a food processor or blender and add the garlic, lemon juice, Worcestershire sauce and one of the anchovy fillets.

4 Blend the mixture until smooth. With the motor running, pour in the olive oil in a thin stream until the dressing has the consistency of single (light) cream.

5 Season the dressing with ground black pepper and a little salt if needed. Pour it over the salad leaves and toss well, then toss in the garlic croûtons, Parmesan cheese and the remaining anchovies and serve immediately.

Warm Chicken Liver Salad

This popular salad makes an excellent light lunch. For a more substantial dish, crumble some roughly chopped pieces of bacon over the salad.

Preparation time 4–5 minutes
Cooking time 4–5 minutes

SERVES 4

115g/4oz each fresh young spinach leaves, rocket (arugula) and lollo rosso lettuce
2 pink grapefruit
90ml/6 tbsp sunflower oil
10ml/2 tsp sesame oil
10ml/2 tsp soy sauce
225g/8oz chicken livers, chopped
salt and ground black pepper

1 Wash, dry and tear up all the spinach and salad leaves. Mix them together well in a large salad bowl. Cut away the peel and white pith from the grapefruit, then segment them, catching the juice in a bowl. Add the segments to the leaves in the bowl.

2 Mix 60ml/4 tbsp sunflower oil with sesame oil, soy sauce and grapefruit juice to taste.

3 Heat the rest of the sunflower oil in a small pan and cook the livers for 4–5 minutes, until firm and lightly browned, stirring occasionally.

4 Tip the chicken livers over the salad. Season the dressing with salt and pepper, drizzle it over the salad and serve immediately.

Thai-Style Cabbage Salad

A simple and delicious way of using cabbage. Broccoli and cauliflower can also be prepared this way.

Preparation time 6 minutes
Cooking time 4 minutes

SERVES 4–6

*30ml/2 tbsp fish sauce
grated rind of 1 lime
30ml/2 tbsp lime juice
120ml/4fl oz/ 1/2 cup coconut milk
30ml/2 tbsp vegetable oil
2 large fresh red chillies, seeded and finely cut into strips
6 garlic cloves, thinly sliced
6 shallots, thinly sliced
1 small cabbage, shredded
30ml/2 tbsp coarsely chopped roasted peanuts, to serve (optional)*

1 Make the dressing. Whisk the fish sauce with the lime rind and juice and coconut milk.

2 Heat the oil in a wok or frying pan. Stir-fry the chillies, garlic and shallots, until the shallots are brown and crisp.

3 Bring a pan of lightly salted water to the boil. Add the cabbage and blanch for about 2 minutes. Drain thoroughly, then tip the cabbage into a bowl.

4 Stir the dressing into the cabbage, toss and mix well. Transfer the salad into a serving dish. Sprinkle with the fried shallot mixture and the coarsely chopped roasted peanuts, if using.

Frisée Lettuce Salad with Bacon

Young dandelion leaves can replace the frisée lettuce and the salad is sometimes sprinkled with chopped hard-boiled egg.

Preparation time 3–4 minutes
Cooking time 6 minutes

SERVES 4

225g/8oz frisée or escarole
  lettuce leaves
75–90ml/5–6 tbsp extra virgin
  olive oil
175g/6oz piece of smoked bacon, diced,
  or 6 thick-cut smoked bacon rashers,
  (strips) cut crossways into thin strips
50g/2oz/1 cup white bread cubes
1 small garlic clove, finely chopped
15ml/1 tbsp red wine vinegar
10ml/2 tsp Dijon mustard
salt and ground black pepper

1 Tear the frisée or escarole lettuce into bite-size pieces and put them in a salad bowl.

COOK'S TIP
Use frisée or escarole leaves as soon as possible after purchase. To store, wrap the leaves in a plastic bag and place in the salad drawer of the refrigerator for up to three days.

2 Heat 15ml/1 tbsp of the oil in a frying pan and add the bacon. Fry until crisp and browned, then remove with a slotted spoon and drain on kitchen paper.

3 Add 30ml/2 tbsp of oil to the pan and fry the bread cubes over a medium-high heat, turning frequently, until evenly browned. Remove with a slotted spoon and drain on kitchen paper.

4 Put the garlic, vinegar and mustard into the pan with the remaining oil and heat until just warm, whisking. Season to taste, then pour over the salad and sprinkle with the fried bacon and croûtons.

GREEN BEAN AND SWEET RED PEPPER SALAD

Preparation time 5–6 minutes
Cooking time Nil

SERVES 4
350g/12oz cooked green
  beans, quartered
2 red (bell) peppers, seeded
  and chopped
2 spring onions (scallions), chopped
1 or more drained pickled serrano
  chillies, rinsed, seeded and chopped
1 iceberg lettuce, coarsely shredded,
  or mixed salad leaves
olives, to garnish
FOR THE DRESSING
45ml/3 tbsp red wine vinegar
135ml/9 tbsp olive oil
salt and ground black pepper

1 Combine the green beans, peppers, spring onions and chillies in a bowl.

2 Make the dressing. Pour the red wine vinegar into a bowl or jug (pitcher). Add salt and ground black pepper to taste, then whisk in the olive oil until well combined.

3 Pour half the salad dressing over the prepared vegetables and toss lightly together to mix and coat thoroughly. Taste the mixture and add more dressing if required. You could also offer it separately.

4 Line a large platter with the shredded lettuce leaves and arrange the dressed vegetable mixture attractively on top. Garnish with the olives and serve, with any extra dressing.

Warm Broad Bean and Feta Salad

This recipe is loosely based on a typical medley of fresh-tasting Greek salad ingredients – broad beans, tomatoes and feta cheese. It's lovely warm or cold as an appetizer or accompaniment.

Preparation time 2 minutes
Cooking time 4–5 minutes

SERVES 4–6

900g/2lb broad (fava) beans, shelled, or 350g/12oz frozen shelled beans
60ml/4 tbsp olive oil
175g/6oz plum tomatoes, halved, or quartered if large
4 garlic cloves, crushed
115g/4oz firm feta cheese, cut into chunks
45ml/3 tbsp chopped fresh dill, plus extra to garnish
12 black olives
salt and ground black pepper

1. Cook the fresh or frozen beans in boiling, salted water until just tender. Drain and set aside.

2. Meanwhile, heat the oil in a heavy frying pan and add the tomatoes and garlic. Cook over a high heat until the tomatoes are beginning to colour.

3. Add the feta to the pan and toss the ingredients together for 1 minute. Tip into a salad bowl and mix with the drained beans, dill, olives and salt and pepper. Serve garnished with chopped dill.

Halloumi and Grape Salad

Halloumi, a cheese used in Greek and Turkish cooking, is delicious fried. Its salty flavour is the ideal foil for grapes and salad greens.

Preparation time 2 minutes
Cooking time 2–3 minutes

SERVES 4

150g/5oz mixed green salad leaves
75g/3oz/¾ cup each seedless green and black grapes
250g/9oz halloumi cheese
45ml/3 tbsp olive oil
fresh young thyme leaves and basil sprigs, to garnish
FOR THE DRESSING
60ml/4 tbsp olive oil
15ml/1 tbsp lemon juice
2.5ml/½ tsp caster (superfine) sugar
salt and ground black pepper
15ml/1 tbsp chopped fresh thyme or dill

1. To make the dressing, whisk together the olive oil, lemon juice and sugar. Season with salt and pepper. Stir in the thyme or dill and set aside.

2. Toss together the salad leaves and the green and black grapes, then transfer to a large serving plate.

3. Thinly slice the cheese. Heat the oil in a large frying pan. Add the cheese and fry briefly until it turns golden on the underside. Turn the cheese with a fish slice (spatula) and cook the other side.

4. Arrange the cheese over the salad. Pour over the dressing and garnish with thyme and basil.

TURKISH SALAD

This classic salad is a wonderful combination of textures and flavours. The saltiness of the cheese is perfectly balanced by the refreshing salad vegetables.

Preparation time 8–10 minutes
Cooking time Nil

SERVES 4
1 cos (romaine) lettuce heart
1 green (bell) pepper
1 red (bell) pepper
½ cucumber
4 tomatoes
1 red onion
225g/8oz feta cheese, crumbled
black olives, to garnish
FOR THE DRESSING
45ml/3 tbsp olive oil
45ml/3 tbsp lemon juice
1 garlic clove, crushed
15ml/1 tbsp chopped fresh parsley
15ml/1 tbsp chopped fresh mint
salt and ground black pepper

1 Chop the lettuce into bite-size pieces. Seed the peppers, remove the cores and cut the flesh into thin strips. Chop the cucumber and slice or chop the tomatoes. Cut the onion in half, then slice finely.

2 Place the chopped lettuce, peppers, cucumber, tomatoes and onion in a large bowl. Sprinkle the feta over the top and toss lightly.

3 Make the dressing. Whisk together the olive oil, lemon juice and garlic in a small bowl. Stir in the chopped fresh parsley and mint and season with salt and ground black pepper to taste.

4 Pour the dressing over the salad, toss lightly and serve immediately, garnished with a handful of black olives.

PERSIAN SALAD

Some of the simplest dishes are also the most successful. This salad is made in minutes and has a crisp, fresh flavour. Serve it with cold meats and baked potatoes.

Preparation time 5 minutes
Cooking time Nil

SERVES 2
4 tomatoes
½ cucumber
1 onion
1 cos (romaine) lettuce heart
FOR THE DRESSING
30ml/2 tbsp olive oil
juice of 1 lemon
1 garlic clove, crushed
salt and ground black pepper

1 Cut the tomatoes and cucumber into small cubes. Finely chop the onion and tear the lettuce into bite-size pieces.

2 Place the tomatoes, cucumber, onion and lettuce in a large salad bowl and mix lightly together.

3 To make the dressing, pour the olive oil into a small bowl. Add the lemon juice and garlic and whisk together well. Stir in salt to taste. Pour over the salad and toss lightly to mix. Sprinkle with black pepper and serve at once.

Summer Noodle Salad with Fragrant Herbs

A refreshing salad with all the tangy flavour of the sea. Try it with squid, scallops, mussels or crab.

Preparation time 8 minutes
Cooking time 1 minute

SERVES 4

115g/4oz cellophane noodles, soaked in hot water until soft
16 cooked prawns (shrimp), peeled
1 small green (bell) pepper, seeded and cut into strips
½ cucumber, cut into strips
1 tomato, cut into strips
2 shallots, thinly sliced
salt and ground black pepper
fresh coriander (cilantro) leaves, to garnish

FOR THE DRESSING

15ml/1 tbsp rice vinegar
30ml/2 tbsp fish sauce
30ml/2 tbsp fresh lime juice
pinch of salt
2.5ml/½ tsp grated fresh root ginger
1 lemon grass stalk, finely chopped
1 fresh red chilli, seeded and sliced
30ml/2 tbsp roughly chopped mint
few sprigs tarragon, roughly chopped
15ml/1 tbsp chopped chives

1 Make the dressing by mixing all the ingredients in a small bowl or jug (pitcher); whisk well.

2 Drain the noodles, then plunge them in a pan of boiling water for 1 minute. Drain, rinse under cold running water and drain again.

3 Combine the noodles with the prawns, pepper, cucumber, tomato and shallots in a bowl. Season with salt and pepper, then toss with the dressing.

4 Spoon the noodle mixture on to individual plates, arranging the prawns on top. Garnish with the coriander leaves and serve.

COOK'S TIPS
Prawns (shrimp) are available ready-cooked and often shelled. To cook raw prawns, boil them for about 5 minutes or until they turn pink. Leave them to cool in the cooking liquid, then remove and gently pull off the tail shell and twist off the head.

Thai Noodle Salad

The addition of coconut milk and sesame oil gives an unusual nutty flavour to the dressing for this colourful, noodle salad.

Preparation time 5 minutes
Cooking time 5 minutes

SERVES 4–6

350g/12oz somen noodles
1 large carrot, cut into thin strips
1 bunch asparagus, trimmed and cut into 4cm/1½ in lengths
1 red (bell) pepper, seeded and cut into fine strips
115g/4oz mangetouts (snow peas), trimmed and halved
115g/4oz baby corn cobs, halved lengthways
115g/4oz beansprouts
115g/4oz can water chestnuts, drained and finely sliced

FOR THE DRESSING
45ml/3 tbsp roughly torn basil leaves
75ml/5 tbsp roughly chopped mint
250ml/8fl oz/1 cup coconut milk
30ml/2 tbsp dark sesame oil
15ml/1 tbsp grated fresh root ginger
2 garlic cloves, finely chopped
juice of 1 lime
2 spring onions (scallions), finely chopped
salt and cayenne pepper

TO GARNISH
1 lime, cut into wedges
50g/2oz/½ cup roasted peanuts, roughly chopped
fresh coriander (cilantro) leaves

VARIATIONS
Garnish with shredded omelette or sliced hard-boiled (hard-cooked) eggs..

1 Make the dressing. Combine the basil, mint, coconut milk, sesame oil, ginger, garlic, lime juice and spring onions in a bowl and mix well. Season to taste with salt and cayenne pepper.

2 Cook the noodles in a large pan of boiling water until just tender, following the directions on the packet.

3 Meanwhile, cook the vegetables in separate pans of boiling salted water until crisp-tender. Drain, plunge them into cold water and drain again. Drain and refresh the noodles in the same way.

4 Toss the noodles, vegetables and dressing together. Arrange on plates and garnish with the lime, peanuts and coriander.

Cabbage Slaw with Date and Apple

Three types of cabbage are shredded together for serving raw, so that the maximum amount of vitamin C is retained in this cheerful and speedy salad.

Preparation time 8 minutes
Cooking time Nil

SERVES 6–8
¼ small white cabbage, shredded
¼ small red cabbage, shredded
¼ small Savoy cabbage, shredded
175g/6oz/1 cup dried stoned (pitted) dates
3 eating apples
juice of 1 lemon
10ml/2 tsp caraway seeds
FOR THE DRESSING
60ml/4 tbsp olive oil
15ml/1 tbsp cider (hard) vinegar
5ml/1 tsp clear honey
salt and ground black pepper

1. Finely shred all the cabbages and place the shredded cabbage in a large salad bowl.

2. Chop the dates and add them to the cabbage.

3. Core the eating apples and slice them thinly into a mixing bowl. Add the lemon juice and toss together to prevent discoloration before adding them to the salad bowl.

4. Make the dressing. Combine the oil, vinegar and honey in a screw-top jar. Add salt and pepper, then close the jar tightly and shake well. Pour the dressing over the salad, toss lightly, then sprinkle with the caraway seeds and toss again.

COOK'S TIPS
Support local orchards by looking out for different home-grown apples. Many delicious, older varieties are grown by specialist farmers, who will willingly offer a taste to would-be buyers. Choose both green- and red-skinned apples if possible, to add extra colour to the salad.

Sprouted Seed Salad

If you sprout beans, lentils and whole grains, this increases their nutritional value, and they make a deliciously crunchy salad.

Preparation time 5 minutes
Cooking time Nil

SERVES 4
2 eating apples
115g/4oz/2 cups alfalfa sprouts
115g/4oz/2 cups beansprouts
115g/4oz/2 cups aduki beansprouts
¼ cucumber, sliced
2 bunches watercress (salad cress), trimmed
FOR THE DRESSING
150ml/¼ pint/⅔ cup low-fat natural (plain) yogurt
juice of ½ lemon
bunch of chives, snipped
30ml/2 tbsp chopped fresh herbs
ground black pepper

1. Core and slice the apples; mix with the other salad ingredients.

2. Whisk the dressing ingredients in a jug (pitcher). Drizzle over the salad and toss just before serving.

COOK'S TIP
You'll find a variety of bean and seed sprouts in the chiller cabinets of large supermarkets and health food shops. They are best used immediately, but will keep in the salad drawer of the refrigerator for a day or two.

Citrus Green Leaf Salad with Croûtons

Wholemeal croûtons add a delicious crunch to leaf salads. The kumquats or orange segments provide a colour contrast as well as a good helping of vitamin C.

Preparation time 4 minutes
Cooking time 1 minute

SERVES 4–6
4 kumquats or 2 seedless oranges
200g/7oz mixed green salad leaves
4 slices of wholemeal (whole-wheat) bread, crusts removed
30–45ml/2–3 tbsp pine nuts, lightly toasted
FOR THE DRESSING
grated rind of 1 lemon
15ml/1 tbsp lemon juice
45ml/3 tbsp olive oil
5ml/1 tsp wholegrain mustard
1 garlic clove, crushed
salt and ground black pepper

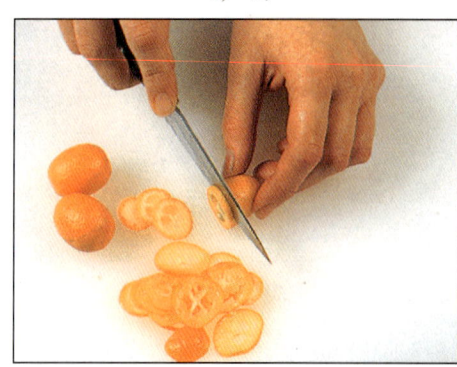

1 Thinly slice the kumquats, or peel and segment the oranges.

COOK'S TIP
Kumquats look like tiny oval oranges. The skin is edible.

2 Tear all the salad leaves into bite-size pieces and mix together in a large salad bowl.

3 Toast the bread on both sides and cut into cubes. Add to the salad leaves with the sliced kumquats or orange segments.

4 Shake all the dressing ingredients together in a jar. Pour over the salad just before serving and scatter the toasted pine nuts over the top.

Mixed Bean Salad with Tomato Dressing

All pulses are a good source of vegetable protein and minerals; this hearty salad makes a meal.

Preparation time 3–4 minutes
Cooking time 5–6 minutes

SERVES 4
115g/4oz green beans
425g/15oz can mixed pulses, drained, rinsed and drained again
2 celery sticks (stalks), finely chopped
1 small onion, finely chopped
3 tomatoes, chopped
chopped fresh parsley, to garnish
FOR THE DRESSING
45ml/3 tbsp olive oil
10ml/2 tsp red wine vinegar
1 garlic clove, crushed
15ml/1 tbsp tomato chutney
salt and ground black pepper

1 Trim the green beans, then cook them in boiling water for 5–6 minutes until tender. Drain, refresh under cold running water, drain again and cut into thirds.

2 Place the beans and mixed pulses in a large bowl. Add the celery, onion and tomatoes and toss well to mix.

3 Shake the dressing ingredients together in a jar. Pour over the salad and sprinkle with the parsley.

COOK'S TIP
Cans of mixed pulses include several different types, such as chickpeas, pinto, black-eyed beans (peas), red kidney, soya beans and azuki beans, and save the hassle of long soaking and cooking that dried beans require.

Spinach with Raisins and Pine Nuts

Raisins and pine nuts are frequent partners in Spanish recipes. Here, tossed with wilted spinach and croûtons, they make a delicious and swiftly prepared snack.

Preparation time 2 minutes
Cooking time 5 minutes

SERVES 4

50g/2oz/⅓ cup raisins
1 thick slice crusty white bread
45ml/3 tbsp olive oil
25g/1oz/¼ cup pine nuts
500g/1¼ lb young spinach leaves, stalks removed
2 garlic cloves, crushed
salt and ground black pepper

1 Put the raisins in a small bowl. Pour over boiling water to cover and set aside to soak while you make the croûtons and prepare the rest of the salad ingredients.

2 Cut the bread into cubes and discard the crusts. Heat 30ml/ 2 tbsp of the oil and fry the bread until golden. Drain.

3 Heat the remaining oil in the pan. Fry the pine nuts until beginning to colour. Add the spinach and garlic and cook quickly, turning the spinach until it has just wilted.

4 Drain the raisins and add them to the pan. Toss gently and season lightly with salt and pepper. Transfer to a warmed serving dish. Scatter with the croûtons and serve the salad at once.

Variations

When you have a little more time, use Swiss chard or spinach beet instead of the spinach. They need to be cooked for slightly longer, but both have very good flavour.

Balti Mushrooms in a Creamy Garlic Sauce

Preparation time 5 minutes
Cooking time 5 minutes

SERVES 4

350g/12oz/3 cups button (white) mushrooms
45ml/3 tbsp olive oil
1 bay leaf
3 garlic cloves, roughly chopped
2 green chillies, seeded and chopped
225g/8oz/1 cup fromage frais or ricotta cheese
15ml/1 tbsp chopped fresh mint
15ml/1 tbsp chopped fresh coriander (cilantro)
5ml/1 tsp salt
fresh mint and coriander (cilantro) leaves, to garnish

1 Unless they are very small, cut the mushrooms in half. Set them aside in a bowl.

2 Heat the oil in a non-stick wok or balti pan, then add the bay leaf, garlic and chillies and cook for about 1 minute.

3 Add the mushrooms. Stir-fry for about 2 minutes.

Cook's Tip
Cook the mushrooms for longer if you like them well cooked and browned.

4 Remove the pan from the heat and stir in the fromage frais or ricotta, mint, coriander and salt. Heat again, stirring for 2 minutes, then transfer to a large warmed serving dish, garnish with the mint and coriander leaves and serve.

VEGETABLE AND EGG NOODLE RIBBONS

Serve this elegant, colourful dish with a tossed green salad as a light lunch. Use fresh pasta for optimum speed and flavour.

Preparation time 3 minutes
Cooking time 7 minutes

SERVES 4
1 large carrot, peeled
2 courgettes (zucchini)
50g/2oz/¼ cup butter
15ml/1 tbsp olive oil
6 fresh shiitake mushrooms, thinly sliced
50g/2oz/½ cup frozen peas, thawed
350g/12oz broad egg ribbon noodles
10ml/2 tsp chopped fresh mixed herbs, such as marjoram, chives and basil
salt and ground black pepper
25g/1oz Parmesan cheese, to serve (optional)

1. Using a vegetable peeler, slice thin strips from the carrot and from the courgettes.

2. Heat the butter with the olive oil in a large frying pan. Stir in the carrots and shiitake mushrooms; fry for 2 minutes. Add the courgettes and peas and stir-fry until the courgettes are cooked, but still crisp. Season with salt and black pepper.

3. Meanwhile, cook the noodles in a large pan of boiling water until just tender. Drain the noodles well and tip them into a bowl. Add the cooked vegetables and toss gently to mix.

4. Sprinkle over the fresh herbs and season to taste. If using the Parmesan cheese, grate or shave it over the top. Toss lightly and serve.

BUCKWHEAT NOODLES WITH GOAT'S CHEESE

When you don't feel like doing a lot of cooking, try this good, fast supper dish. The earthy flavour of buckwheat goes well with the nutty, peppery taste of rocket, and both are offset by the deliciously creamy goat's cheese.

Preparation and cooking time 8–10 minutes

SERVES 4
350g/12oz buckwheat noodles
50g/2oz/¼ cup butter
2 garlic cloves, finely chopped
4 shallots, sliced
75g/3oz/¾ cup hazelnuts, lightly roasted and roughly chopped
large handful rocket (arugula) leaves
175g/6oz goat's cheese
salt and ground black pepper

1. Bring a large pan of lightly salted water to a rolling boil and add the buckwheat noodles. Cook until just tender.

2. Meanwhile, heat the butter in a large frying pan. Add the garlic and shallots and cook for 2–3 minutes, stirring constantly, until the shallots are soft. Do not let the garlic brown.

3. Drain the noodles well. Add the hazelnuts to the pan and fry for about 1 minute. Add the rocket leaves and, when they start to wilt, toss in the cooked noodles and stir to heat through.

4. Season with salt and pepper. Crumble in the goat's cheese and serve immediately.

Melon and Strawberry Salad

A beautiful and colourful fruit salad, this is a particularly good dessert to serve after a spicy main course. For speed, cube the melons.

Preparation time 8–10 minutes
Cooking time Nil

SERVES 4
1 cantaloupe melon
1 honeydew melon
½ watermelon
225g/8oz/2 cups fresh strawberries
15ml/1 tbsp lemon juice
15ml/1 tbsp clear honey
15ml/1 tbsp water
15ml/1 tbsp chopped fresh mint
1 mint sprig, to garnish (optional)

1. Prepare the melons by cutting them in half and discarding the seeds. Use a melon baller to scoop out the flesh into balls, or cut it into cubes with a knife. Place the melon balls (or cubes) in a fruit bowl.

2. Rinse and hull the stems of the strawberries, cut them in half and add them to the fruit bowl.

3. Mix together the lemon juice, clear honey and water. Stir carefully to blend and then pour over the fruit. Stir the fruit so that it is thoroughly coated in the lemon and honey mixture.

4. Sprinkle the chopped mint over the top of the fruit. Serve garnished with the mint sprig, if you like.

COOK'S TIP
Use whichever melons are available: substitute charentais for watermelon, for example. However, try to find three different kinds of melon so that you get variation in colour, and also a variety of textures and flavours.

FIGS WITH RICOTTA CREAM

Fresh, ripe figs are full of natural sweetness, and need little adornment. This simple recipe makes the most of their beautiful, intense flavour.

Preparation time 3–4 minutes
Cooking time Nil

SERVES 4
4 ripe, fresh figs
115g/4oz/½ cup ricotta or cottage cheese
45ml/3 tbsp crème fraîche
15ml/1 tbsp clear honey
2.5ml/½ tsp vanilla essence (extract)
freshly grated nutmeg, to decorate

1. Trim the stalks from the figs. Make four cuts through each fig from the stalk-end, cutting them almost through but leaving them joined at the base.

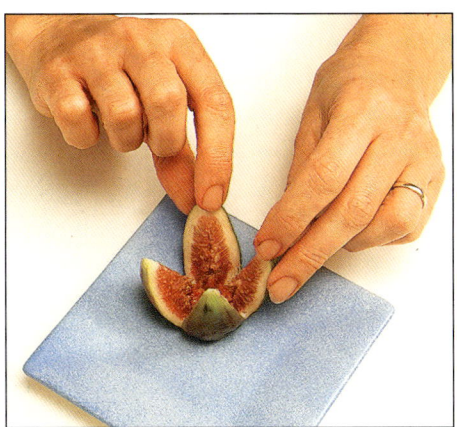

2. Place the figs on serving plates and ease the cuts apart gently to open them out.

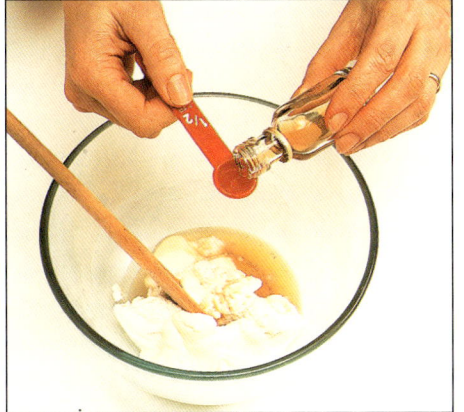

3. Mix together the ricotta or cottage cheese, crème fraîche, honey and vanilla essence.

VARIATION
Use full-fat soft cheese instead and Greek (US strained plain) yogurt in place of the crème fraîche.

4. Spoon a little ricotta cream on to each plate and sprinkle with grated nutmeg to serve.

Emerald Fruit Salad

The cool, green-coloured fruits make a refreshing and fast dessert.

Preparation and cooking time 8 minutes

SERVES 4
30ml/2 tbsp lime juice
30ml/2 tbsp clear honey
2 green eating apples, cored
  and sliced
1 small ripe melon, diced
2 kiwi fruit, sliced
1 star fruit, sliced
fresh mint sprigs, to decorate
yogurt or fromage frais, to serve

1 Mix together the lime juice and honey in a large bowl, then toss the apple slices in this.

2 Stir in the melon, kiwi fruit and star fruit. Place in a glass serving dish.

3 Decorate the fruit salad with mint sprigs and serve with yogurt or fromage frais.

VARIATIONS
Add other green fruits when available, such as greengages, grapes, pears or kiwano, which is a type of melon. It has a tough yellowy-orange rind covered with sharp spikes, and the flesh inside looks like a bright green jelly, encasing edible seeds, which can be removed with a spoon. If time permits, chill the salad for an hour or two before serving. It is delicious with extra-thick cream to which a couple of spoonfuls of advocaat or eggnog have been added.

Warm Bagels with Poached Apricots

Preparation time 2 minutes
Cooking time 8 minutes

SERVES 4

*a few strips of orange peel
225g/8oz/1⅓ cups ready-to-eat
  dried apricots
250ml/8fl oz/1 cup orange juice
2.5ml/½ tsp orange flower water
2 cinnamon and raisin bagels
20ml/4 tsp orange marmalade
60ml/4 tbsp crème fraîche or
  sour cream
15g/½oz/2 tbsp chopped pistachio
  nuts, to decorate*

1 Cut the strips of orange peel into fine shreds. Cook them in boiling water until softened, then drain and place in cold water.

2 Preheat the oven to 160°C/325°F/Gas 3. Combine the apricots and orange juice in a small pan. Simmer for about 6 minutes until the juice has reduced and looks syrupy. Set aside to cool, then stir in the orange flower water. Meanwhile, place the bagels on a baking sheet and warm in the oven for about 5–10 minutes.

3 Split the bagels in half horizontally. Lay one half, crumb uppermost, on each serving plate. Spread 5ml/1 tsp orange marmalade on each bagel.

4 Spoon 15ml/1 tbsp crème fraîche or sour cream into the centre of each bagel and place a quarter of the apricot compôte at the side. Scatter orange peel and pistachio nuts over the top to decorate. Serve immediately.

Cook's Tip
When you remove the strips of rind from the orange, use a swivel-action vegetable peeler to obtain thin strips and avoid removing any of the bitter white pith with the rind.

Brazilian Coffee Bananas

Preparation time 4 minutes
Cooking time Nil

SERVES 4

4 small ripe bananas
15ml/1 tbsp instant coffee granules (powder)
15ml/1 tbsp hot water
30ml/2 tbsp dark muscovado (molasses) sugar
250g/9oz/generous 1 cup Greek (US strained plain) yogurt
15ml/1 tbsp toasted flaked (sliced) almonds

1 Peel and slice one banana and mash the remaining three with a fork. Set the sliced banana aside.

2 Dissolve the coffee granules in the hot water and stir into the mashed bananas.

3 Spoon a little of the mashed banana mixture into four serving dishes and sprinkle with the muscovado sugar. Top with a spoonful of yogurt, then repeat until all the ingredients are used up.

4 Swirl the last layer of yogurt for a marbled effect. Finish with a few banana slices and the flaked almonds. Serve immediately, or the bananas will discolour.

Hot Bananas with Rum and Raisins

Choose almost-ripe bananas with evenly coloured skins, either all yellow or just green at the tips.

Preparation time 2 minutes
Cooking time 3–4 minutes

SERVES 4
40g/1½oz/¼ cup seedless raisins
75ml/5 tbsp dark rum
50g/2oz/¼ cup unsalted (sweet) butter
60ml/4 tbsp soft light brown sugar
4 ripe bananas, peeled and halved lengthways
1.5ml/¼ tsp grated nutmeg
1.5ml/¼ tsp ground cinnamon
30ml/2 tbsp slivered almonds, toasted
chilled cream, to serve (optional)

1. Put the raisins in a bowl with the rum. Set aside to soak while you fry the bananas.

2. Melt the butter in a frying pan, add the sugar and stir until dissolved. Add the bananas and cook for a few minutes until tender.

3. Sprinkle the spices over the bananas, then pour over the rum and raisins. Carefully set alight using a long taper and stir gently.

4. Sprinkle over the slivered almonds and serve immediately with chilled cream, if using.

Eton Mess

This dish is traditionally enjoyed by parents and pupils on the lawns at the annual prize-giving at Eton College, England.

Preparation time 7 minutes
Cooking time Nil

SERVES 4
500g/1¼lb/5 cups strawberries, chopped
45–60ml/3–4 tbsp Kirsch
300ml/½ pint/1¼ cups double (heavy) cream
6 small white meringues
fresh mint sprigs, to decorate

1. Put the strawberries in a bowl, sprinkle over the Kirsch, then set aside for 3–4 minutes.

2. Whip the cream until soft peaks form, then gently fold in the strawberries with their juices.

3. Crush the meringues into rough chunks, then scatter over the strawberry mixture and fold in gently.

4. Spoon the strawberry mixture into a glass serving bowl, decorate with fresh mint sprigs and serve immediately.

COOK'S TIP
If you would prefer to make a slightly less rich version, use Greek (US strained plain) yogurt or thick natural (plain) yogurt instead of part or all of the cream. Simply beat the yogurt gently before adding the strawberry and Kirsch mixture.

Ice Cream Strawberry Shortcake

This dessert is an American classic, and couldn't be easier. Fresh juicy strawberries, store-bought flan cases and rich ice cream are all you need to create a creamy dessert.

Preparation time 10 minutes
Cooking time Nil

SERVES 4

3 x 15cm/6in ready-made sponge cake flan cases or shortbreads
675g/1½lb/6 cups strawberries
1.2 litres/2 pints/5 cups vanilla or strawberry ice cream
icing (confectioners') sugar, for dusting

[1] If using sponge cake flan cases, trim the raised edges with a serrated knife.

[2] Hull and halve the strawberries. Spoon one-third of the ice cream on to a flan case or shortbread layer, placing it in scoops, with one-third of the strawberries in between.

[3] Spoon more strawberries and ice cream on to a second flan or shortbread layer and place it on top of the first, then add the final layer, piling the strawberries up high.

Cook's Tips
Don't worry if the shortcake falls apart a little when you cut into it. It may look messy, but it will taste marvellous. If time permits, the dessert can be assembled up to an hour before serving and kept in the freezer without spoiling the fruit.

Mandarins in Orange Flower Syrup

You can cheat with this recipe and buy canned whole peeled mandarins or clementines. Use fresh orange juice for the syrup. You can serve immediately, but it is better chilled.

Preparation time 10 minutes
Cooking time Nil

SERVES 4
10 mandarins
15ml/1 tbsp icing (confectioners') sugar
10ml/2 tsp orange flower water
15ml/1 tbsp chopped pistachio nuts

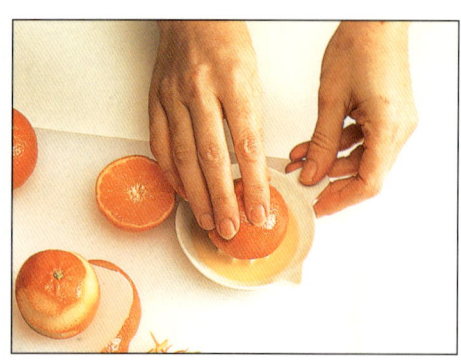

1 Thinly pare a little of the coloured rind from one of the mandarins and cut it into fine shreds for decoration. Squeeze the juice from two mandarins and reserve it.

2 Peel the remaining fruit, removing as much of the white pith as possible. Arrange the whole fruit in a wide dish.

3 Mix the reserved juice, sugar and orange flower water and pour it over the fruit. Cover the dish and chill for 5 minutes.

4 Meanwhile, blanch the shreds of rind in boiling water for 30 seconds. Drain and set aside to cool. Sprinkle them over the mandarins, with the pistachio nuts before serving.

Papaya Skewers with Passion Fruit Coulis

Fresh-tasting tropical fruits, full of sweetness, make a simple dessert.

Preparation time 7–8 minutes
Cooking time Nil

SERVES 6
3 ripe papayas
10 passion fruit or kiwi fruit
30ml/2 tbsp lime juice
30ml/2 tbsp icing (confectioners') sugar
30ml/2 tbsp white rum
lime slices, to decorate

1. Cut the papayas in half and scoop out the seeds. Peel them and cut the flesh into even-size chunks. Thread the chunks on to six bamboo skewers.

2. Cut eight of the passion fruit in half and scoop out the flesh with a teaspoon. Purée the flesh for a few seconds in a blender or food processor. If using kiwi fruit, slice off the top and bottom from eight of the fruits, then remove the skin. Cut the kiwi fruit in half and purée them briefly.

3. Press the pulp through a sieve (strainer) placed over a bowl and discard the seeds. Add the lime juice, sugar and rum, and stir until the sugar has dissolved.

4. Spoon a little coulis on to six serving plates. Arrange the skewers on top. Scoop the flesh from the remaining passion fruit and spoon it over or slice the kiwi fruit and add it. Decorate with the lime slices.

COOK'S TIP
If you are short of time, the passion fruit flesh can be used as it is, without puréeing or sieving (straining). Simply scoop the flesh from the skins and mix it with the lime, sugar and rum. Kiwi fruit will still need to be puréed.

Quick Apricot Blender Whip

This is one of the quickest and prettiest desserts you could make.

Preparation time 4 minutes
Cooking time 2 minutes

SERVES 4
400g/14oz can apricot halves in juice
15ml/1 tbsp Grand Marnier or brandy
175ml/6fl oz/¾ cup Greek (US strained plain) yogurt
30ml/2 tbsp flaked (sliced) almonds

COOK'S TIP
For an even lighter dessert, use low-fat yogurt, and, if you prefer to omit the liqueur, add a little of the fruit juice from the can.

1 Drain the juice from the canned apricot halves and place the fruit in a blender or food processor with the liqueur.

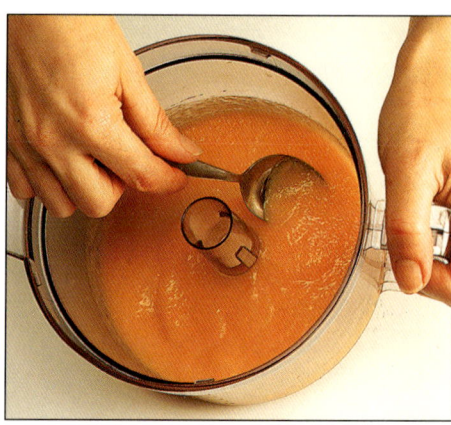

2 Process the apricots until they are smooth.

3 Spoon the fruit purée and yogurt in alternate spoonfuls into four tall glasses or glass dishes, swirling them together slightly to give a marbled effect.

4 Lightly toast the almonds until they are golden. Let them cool slightly and then sprinkle some on top of each dessert.

Raspberry and Passion Fruit Swirls

If passion fruit is not available, just use extra raspberries.

Preparation time 4–5 minutes
Cooking time Nil

SERVES 4

400g/14oz/1¾ cups low-fat
 fromage frais or ricotta cheese
30ml/2 tbsp caster (superfine) sugar
2 passion fruit
300g/11oz/2 cups raspberries
raspberries and sprigs of mint,
 to decorate

1 Put the fromage frais and sugar in a bowl. Scoop out the passion fruit pulp and add it to the bowl. Mash the raspberries in a separate bowl until the juice runs.

2 Spoon alternate spoonfuls of the raspberry pulp and the fromage frais or ricotta cheese mixture into small individual bowls, stemmed glasses or one large serving dish.

3 Stir lightly to create a gentle swirled effect. Decorate each dessert with a raspberry and a sprig of fresh mint. Serve immediately.

Cook's Tip
Over-ripe, slightly soft fruit can also be used in this recipe. You could use frozen raspberries when fresh are not available, but thaw them first.

Variation
Other summer fruits could be used – try a mix of strawberries and redcurrants with the raspberries, or use peeled and stoned (pitted) mangoes, peaches or apricots, which you will need to purée before mixing with the fromage frais or ricotta cheese.

Italian Ricotta Pudding

This creamy, rich dessert is very easy to make. Ideally, it should be chilled before serving, but it can be served within minutes of making. Just pop it in the freezer while you eat your main course.

Preparation time 5–6 minutes
Cooking time Nil

SERVES 4–6
225g/8oz/1 cup ricotta cheese
50g/2oz/⅓ cup candied fruits
60ml/4 tbsp sweet Marsala
250ml/8fl oz/1 cup double (heavy) cream
50g/2oz/¼ cup caster (superfine) sugar, plus extra to serve
finely grated rind of 1 orange
350g/12oz/2 cups fresh raspberries
strips of thinly pared orange rind, to decorate

1. Press the ricotta through a sieve (strainer) into a bowl. Finely chop the candied fruits and stir into the ricotta with half the Marsala. Put the cream, sugar and orange rind in another bowl and whip until the cream is standing in soft peaks.

2. Fold the whipped cream into the ricotta mixture. Spoon into individual glass serving bowls and top with the raspberries.

3. Sprinkle the raspberries with the remaining Marsala and dust the top of each dessert liberally with caster sugar. Decorate with the strips of pared orange rind and serve.

COOK'S TIP
Buy candied fruits in large pieces from a good delicatessen – tubs of chopped candied peel are too tough to eat raw, and should only be used in baking.

Chocolate Fudge Sundaes

Preparation time 3 minutes
Cooking time 6 minutes

SERVES 4
4 scoops each vanilla and coffee ice cream
2 small ripe bananas, sliced
whipped cream
toasted flaked (sliced) almonds
FOR THE SAUCE
50g/2oz/⅓ cup soft light brown sugar
120ml/4fl oz/½ cup golden (light corn) syrup
45ml/3 tbsp strong black coffee
5ml/1 tsp ground cinnamon
150g/5oz plain (semisweet) chocolate, chopped
75ml/3fl oz/⅓ cup whipping cream

1 To make the sauce, bring the sugar, syrup, coffee and cinnamon to the boil in a heavy pan and boil for 5 minutes, stirring.

2 Turn off the heat, leave to cool for 1 minute, then stir in the chopped chocolate. When melted and smooth, stir in the cream. Set aside to cool a little while you assemble the sundaes.

3 Fill four tall glasses with a small scoop each of vanilla and coffee ice cream.

4 Scatter the sliced bananas over the ice cream. Pour the warm fudge sauce over the bananas, then top each sundae with a generous swirl of whipped cream. Sprinkle with toasted flaked almonds and serve immediately.

VARIATIONS
Ring the changes by choosing other flavours of ice cream. Strawberry, toffee or chocolate work well. In the summer, substitute raspberries or strawberries for the bananas, and sprinkle chopped roasted hazelnuts on top in place of the flaked (sliced) almonds.

Index

A
apricots: quick apricot blender whip, 92
  warm bagels with poached apricots, 85
asparagus: with tarragon butter, 26
avgolemono, 16

B
bacon: frisée salad with, 66
  spinach salad with prawns and, 62
bagels, warm, with poached apricots, 85
bananas: Brazilian coffee, 86
  with rum and raisins, 87
beans: mixed bean salad with tomato dressing, 76

C
cabbage: slaw with date and apple, 74
  Thai-style cabbage salad, 65
calf's liver with honey, 42
cheese: buckwheat noodles with goat's cheese, 80
  ciabatta with mozzarella and onion, 31
  French goat's cheese salad 60
  halloumi and grape salad, 68
  hot tomato and mozzarella salad, 26
  melting cheese dip, 30
  pork with Camembert, 44
  ravioli with four-cheese sauce, 57
  salad leaves with Gorgonzola, 32
  tomato and mozzarella toasts, 32
  warm broad bean and feta salad, 68
chicken: cashew chicken, 34
  stir-fried chicken with basil and chillies, 35
  Thai chicken and vegetable stir-fry, 36
  with tomatoes and olives, 37
chocolate: chocolate fudge sundaes, 95
  chocolate sauce, 11
chorizo in olive oil, 22
ciabatta with mozzarella and onion, 31
conchiglie from Pisa, 53

E
emerald fruit salad, 84
Eton mess, 88

F
figs with ricotta cream, 83
frisée lettuce salad with bacon, 66

G
grapefruit: melon and grapefruit cocktail, 20
green bean and sweet red pepper salad, 67
guacamole, 28

H
halibut with tomato vinaigrette, 46
halloumi and grape salad, 68
hummus, 29

I
ice cream: chocolate fudge sundaes, 95
  ice cream strawberry shortcake, 89

L
liver: calf's liver with honey, 42
  pan-fried chicken liver salad, 18
  warm chicken liver salad, 64

M
mandarins in orange flower syrup, 90
mangoes: prosciutto with mango, 20
melon: melon and grapefruit cocktail, 20
  melon and strawberry salad, 82
  melon, pineapple and grape cocktail, 24
mushrooms: balti mushrooms in a creamy garlic sauce, 79

N
noodles: buckwheat noodles with goat's cheese, 80
  buckwheat noodles with smoked salmon, 54
  summer noodle salad with fragrant herbs, 72
  Thai noodle salad, 73
  vegetable and egg noodle ribbons, 80
  with pineapple, ginger and chillies, 54

P
papaya: skewers with passion fruit coulis, 91
pineapple: melon, pineapple and grape cocktail, 24
pork: in sweet-and-sour sauce, 43
  with Camembert, 44

prawns: garlic prawns, 22
  garlicky scallops and prawns, 50
  green prawn curry, 49
  prawn and vegetable balti, 48
prosciutto with mango, 20

R
raspberries: raspberry and passion fruit swirls, 93
ravioli with four-cheese sauce, 57
ricotta: Italian ricotta pudding, 94

S
salads: Caesar, 63
  citrus green leaf salad, 76
  French goat's cheese, 60
  frisée salad with bacon, 66
  Greek salad pittas, 60
  green bean and sweet red pepper, 67
  halloumi and grape, 68
  mixed bean salad with tomato dressing, 76
  pan-fried chicken liver, 18
  Persian, 70
  salad leaves with Gorgonzola, 32
  smoked trout, 25
  spinach with bacon and prawns, 62
  sprouted seed, 74
  summer noodle salad with fragrant herbs, 72
  Thai noodle, 73
  Thai-style cabbage, 65
  Turkish, 70
  warm broad bean and feta, 68
salmon: with green peppercorns, 45
scallops: sautéed scallops, 50
shrimp see prawns
sole: pan-fried with lemon butter sauce, 47
soup: Thai-style corn, 17
spaghetti: alla carbonara, 58
  with rocket pesto, 52
spinach with raisins and pine nuts, 78

T
tagliarini: spinach tagliarini with asparagus, 59
tagliatelle: with prosciutto and asparagus, 56
turkey: crumbed with capers, 38

V
veal: with lemon and vermouth, 39
  pan-fried veal chops, 40
  with tarragon sauce, 40

W
whitebait, deep-fried, 19